Smoking

Other books in the Current Controversies series:

Smoking

Auriana Ojeda, *Book Editor*

Daniel Leone, *President*
Bonnie Szumski, *Publisher*
Scott Barbour, *Managing Editor*

CURRENT CONTROVERSIES

GREENHAVEN PRESS
SAN DIEGO, CALIFORNIA

GALE GROUP

THOMSON LEARNING

Detroit • New York • San Diego • San Francisco
Boston • New Haven, Conn. • Waterville, Maine
London • Munich

Cover photo: Corbis

Library of Congress Cataloging-in-Publication Data

Smoking / Auriana Ojeda, book editor.
     p. cm. — (Current controversies)
    Includes bibliographical references and index.
    ISBN 0-7377-0856-5 (pbk. : alk. paper) — ISBN 0-7377-0857-3
(lib. : alk. paper)
    1. Smoking. I. Ojeda, Auriana, 1977– II. Series.

HV5733.S66   2002
363.4—dc21   2001051247

Copyright © 2002 by Greenhaven Press,
an imprint of The Gale Group
10911 Technology Place, San Diego, CA 92127
Printed in the U.S.A.

Contents

cer and coronary heart disease than cigarette smokers because they neither smoke as frequently nor inhale as deeply. Smoking an occasional cigar does not pose serious health risks.

No: Smoking Is Harmful

Chapter 2: Does Advertising by Tobacco Companies Influence People to Smoke?

Chapter 3: Should Smoking Be Regulated by the Government?

Yes: The Government Should Regulate Smoking

> The tobacco companies have escaped regulation by the Food and Drug
> Administration, although the FDA maintains authority over the testing,
> marketing, and labeling of many less dangerous products. Because
> tobacco and nicotine are unhealthy and addictive substances, the FDA
> should have the authority to regulate them in a manner similar to food
> and prescription drugs.

> Government efforts are necessary to curb youth smoking and to hold the
> tobacco companies accountable for the problems they cause smokers and
> society. Congress should enact legislation imposing such measures as
> severe restrictions on advertising by tobacco companies, higher taxes on
> cigarettes, and efforts to reduce youth smoking through antismoking
> advertisements and stronger enforcement of youth tobacco-access laws.

No: Smoking Should Not Be Regulated by the Government

> Antismoking crusaders contend that smoking is a public health problem,
> but in reality it is only a problem for the individual smoker. The right
> to smoke is a personal choice, and it should not be regulated by the
> government.

> Government efforts to restrict tobacco advertising, require tobacco com-
> panies to fund antismoking campaigns, and strengthen youth tobacco con-
> trols intrude on people's private choice to smoke. Regulation of smoking
> reflects the increasingly intrusive hand of government in personal lives.

> Some contend that increasing taxes on cigarettes will lead to a decrease in
> smoking and a subsequent improvement in public health. There is no
> proof that raising taxes on cigarettes will lead to a reduction in smoking.
> Moreover, because the lower classes make up the majority of smokers,
> higher taxes will unfairly target the poor.

Chapter 4: How Can Smoking Be Reduced?

Foreword

By definition, controversies are "discussions of questions in which opposing opinions clash" (Webster's Twentieth Century Dictionary Unabridged). Few would deny that controversies are a pervasive part of the human condition and exist on virtually every level of human enterprise. Controversies transpire between individuals and among groups, within nations and between nations. Controversies supply the grist necessary for progress by providing challenges and challengers to the status quo. They also create atmospheres where strife and warfare can flourish. A world without controversies would be a peaceful world; but it also would be, by and large, static and prosaic.

The Series' Purpose

The purpose of the Current Controversies series is to explore many of the social, political, and economic controversies dominating the national and international scenes today. Titles selected for inclusion in the series are highly focused and specific. For example, from the larger category of criminal justice, Current Controversies deals with specific topics such as police brutality, gun control, white collar crime, and others. The debates in Current Controversies also are presented in a useful, timeless fashion. Articles and book excerpts included in each title are selected if they contribute valuable, long-range ideas to the overall debate. And wherever possible, current information is enhanced with historical documents and other relevant materials. Thus, while individual titles are current in focus, every effort is made to ensure that they will not become quickly outdated. Books in the Current Controversies series will remain important resources for librarians, teachers, and students for many years.

In addition to keeping the titles focused and specific, great care is taken in the editorial format of each book in the series. Book introductions and chapter prefaces are offered to provide background material for readers. Chapters are organized around several key questions that are answered with diverse opinions representing all points on the political spectrum. Materials in each chapter include opinions in which authors clearly disagree as well as alternative opinions in which authors may agree on a broader issue but disagree on the possible solutions. In this way, the content of each volume in Current Controversies mirrors the mosaic of opinions encountered in society. Readers will quickly realize that there are many viable answers to these complex issues. By questioning each author's conclusions, students and casual readers can begin to develop the critical thinking skills so important to evaluating opinionated material.

Current Controversies is also ideal for controlled research. Each anthology in the series is composed of primary sources taken from a wide gamut of informational categories including periodicals, newspapers, books, United States and foreign government documents, and the publications of private and public organizations. Readers will find factual support for reports, debates, and research papers covering all areas of important issues. In addition, an annotated table of contents, an index, a book and periodical bibliography, and a list of organizations to contact are included in each book to expedite further research.

Perhaps more than ever before in history, people are confronted with diverse and contradictory information. During the Persian Gulf War, for example, the public was not only treated to minute-to-minute coverage of the war, it was also inundated with critiques of the coverage and countless analyses of the factors motivating U.S. involvement. Being able to sort through the plethora of opinions accompanying today's major issues, and to draw one's own conclusions, can be a complicated and frustrating struggle. It is the editors' hope that Current Controversies will help readers with this struggle.

Introduction

In November 1998, forty-six states, the District of Columbia, and five U.S. territories signed the Master Settlement Agreement (MSA) with the five largest tobacco manufacturers (Brown & Williamson, Lorillard, Philip Morris, R.J. Reynolds, Commonwealth, and Liggett & Myers). The main purpose of the settlement was to resolve all lawsuits filed by the state attorneys general that sought to recover the Medicaid costs of treating smokers. The agreement ordered the tobacco companies to make annual payments to the states totaling $206 billion by 2025. It also imposed severe restrictions on the advertising, marketing, and promotion of tobacco products and prohibited marketing such products to youths. According to the Philip Morris tobacco company, "[The tobacco settlement] addresses many of the fundamental controversies that have marked the tobacco 'wars' for decades: youth smoking, corporate accountability for a risky, albeit legal, consumer product, and creating the kind of meaningful change that governments and the public health community have sought. The tobacco settlement agreement has fundamentally changed cigarette marketing and has placed the marketing and lobbying activities of the tobacco industry under a new level of state government and restrictions."

Health advocates have long lobbied for government restrictions over the tobacco industry because of the known health risks associated with smoking, such as various cancers, emphysema, bronchitis, asthma, and heart disease. According to the Centers for Disease Control and Prevention (CDC), tobacco is the leading cause of preventable death in the United States and results in more than 400,000 deaths per year—killing more people than AIDS, alcohol, drug abuse, car accidents, murders, suicides, and fires combined. The CDC maintains that smoking results in more than $50 billion annually in direct medical costs. Even though the surgeon general declared nicotine an addictive drug in 1988, tobacco is not under the jurisdiction of the Food and Drug Administration (FDA) and is therefore not subjected to the same testing and marketing regulations as other drugs or food products.

Antitobacco activists maintain that the FDA should regulate tobacco because the addictive nature of nicotine hooks smokers as adolescents and makes it difficult for them to quit as adults. The CDC maintains that about 80 percent of smokers started smoking before the age of eighteen and that three thousand children each day become smokers. These young smokers get addicted because when they inhale smoke from a cigarette, nicotine is absorbed through their bloodstreams and quickly reaches nerve-cell "nicotine-receptors" in their brains. Nicotine causes the secretion of the neurotransmitters dopamine (inducing feelings of pleasure), norepinephrine (energy and alertness), and endorphins (pain relief and relaxation), which contribute to a pleasant sense of composure. This mild euphoria is short-lived, however, and smokers must smoke more cigarettes more frequently to attain the same "high" they got when they first started smoking. Once a smoker is addicted, the high level of availability, relative lack of negative legal and social ramifications, and the marketing and advertising methods of tobacco companies make quitting extremely difficult, according to the National Institute on Drug Abuse. Every year approximately 35 million smokers try to quit smoking, and fewer than 7 percent of smokers who try to quit on their own succeed.

Many claim that in order to get teens to start smoking, the advertising and marketing practices of tobacco companies target children by portraying cigarette smoking as glamorous, sexy, rebellious, and independent—attributes that appeal to developing adolescents. As evidence, they cite the following advice the New York Advertising Agency presented to a tobacco company in 1975 on how to reach teenagers: "In the young smoker's mind, a cigarette falls into the same category with wine, beer, shaving, wearing a bra (or purposely not wearing one), declaration of independence and striving for self-identity. . . . Thus, an attempt to reach young smokers, starters, should be based, among others, on the following major parameters: Present the cigarette as one of the few initiations into the adult world; Present the cigarette as part of the illicit pleasure category of products and activities."

In response to concerns over the impact of tobacco advertising on children and teens, the 1998 tobacco settlement initiated the most stringent tobacco marketing and advertisement restrictions to date. It banned cartoon characters in advertisements, brand-name sponsorship of events with significant youth audiences, and billboard and sports arena advertising. Tobacco companies are prohibited from marketing to minors or in publications with many youth readers, and they are forbidden to distribute free samples of tobacco products. Some antitobacco forces perceive the settlement agreement as being too lenient, but others consider it a positive step toward more tobacco control and fewer smokers.

Tobacco companies argue that their marketing and advertising practices are not geared toward recruiting new and underage smokers, but are instead intended to gain and retain the business of confirmed adult smokers. According to Philip Morris, "All of our cigarette brand advertising and promotions are intended for adults who choose to smoke. They serve to enhance brand awareness, recognition, and loyalty among adult smokers." Tobacco companies claim that they strive to improve sales by ensuring that the public is aware of the many different brands of cigarettes available, as sales figures prove that the most widely advertised cigarettes are the best sellers. According to Brown & Williamson, "To understand what advertising does *not* do, it is helpful to understand what it *does* accomplish. The purpose of advertising is to contribute to the overall 'equity' of a brand, which is the most important characteristic that a brand possesses. Equity means all that a brand represents to a consumer and is comprised of the product characteristics, the brand image and the user image. . . . The foremost role of cigarette marketing activities is to *influence brand choice.*"

Although the MSA resolved many of the legal issues surrounding smoking and the tobacco companies, controversy regarding advertising restrictions and smoking regulations persists. These issues and others are discussed in *Smoking: Current Controversies*. Contributors to this anthology debate the risks of smoking, the role of advertising in encouraging people to smoke, tobacco regulation, and methods for reducing smoking. Readers will be provided with a clear understanding of the social and policy debates surrounding smoking and tobacco.

Chapter 1

Are the Health Risks of Smoking Exaggerated?

The Health Risks of Secondhand Smoke: An Overview

by Sheryl Stölberg

About the author: *Sheryl Stölberg is the former medical writer for the* Los Angeles Times *and is currently a health writer for the* New York Times.

He wanted his wife to quit smoking.

It was a simple wish, yet its consequences were profound. This was in the 1970s, in Greece, where smoking was as cherished a pastime as baseball in America. Dimitrios Trichopoulos didn't care about bucking the tide. He simply detested his wife's addiction.

A young cancer epidemiologist at the University of Athens, Trichopoulos tried the usual guilt trip. He told her she was hurting herself. On this, he said, the medical literature was clear. When that didn't work, he told her she was hurting him—an argument he could not support with statistics. She didn't believe it.

Ever the scientist, he set out to prove it.

That family argument wound up earning Trichopoulos a place in tobacco history. He was the first researcher to connect secondhand cigarette smoke with an increased risk of lung cancer.

He accomplished this in a somewhat unorthodox fashion, pirating $50,000 from one of his grants to conduct a survey of 189 nonsmoking women. (Greek officials, Trichopoulos says, would never have given him money to study the detrimental effects of a cash crop as lucrative as tobacco.) He found that smokers' wives were twice as likely to develop lung cancer as women married to nonsmokers.

It worked. "I convinced her," Trichopoulos says. His wife quit.

The study did much more than clean the air in the Trichopoulos home. He published it in 1981, days before the publication of a larger study conducted by

Japanese epidemiologist Takeshi Hirayama. These papers gave a huge boost to a grass-roots anti-smoking campaign that has dramatically changed the way Americans work, dine, travel and raise children.

The Secondhand Smoke Revolution

This is the nature of the secondhand smoke revolution: a little bit of science —still emerging, not all of it conclusive—shaping a lot of public policy.

For anti-smoking activists, scientific research into the dangers of secondhand smoke has been a godsend. The high point came in 1993, when the U.S. Environmental Protection Agency declared secondhand smoke a "Group A" human carcinogen, reporting that it accounts for 3,000 lung cancer deaths each year. This placed it in the same deadly category as asbestos and radon; the agency concluded that the danger cannot be eliminated by using smoking and non-smoking sections.

Thanks in large part to that report, secondhand smoke is now one of the nation's most pressing and divisive public health issues. Coupled with allegations that tobacco companies have misrepresented the nicotine content in cigarettes—and tobacco executives' denials—the issue is bringing public outrage to new heights.

But the tobacco industry is fighting back—hard. A coalition of farmers and manufacturers filed a lawsuit alleging that the EPA "manipulated and cherry-picked scientific data" and asked that a U.S. District Court judge in North Carolina nullify the report. In California, tobacco giant Philip Morris has placed a controversial initiative on the November 1994 ballot that would undo local ordinances designed to curb secondhand smoke and replace them with a looser standard.

> *"This is the nature of the secondhand smoke revolution: a little bit of science—still emerging, not all of it conclusive—shaping a lot of public policy."*

And in May 1994, cigarette maker R.J. Reynolds launched an aggressive public information campaign designed to stave off smoking bans by countering the widespread perception that secondhand smoke is dangerous. The company's tactic: Fight science with science.

In full-page newspaper ads, R.J. Reynolds says its research shows that nonsmokers are exposed to "very little" secondhand smoke, even when they live or work with smokers. In one month, the company said, a nonsmoker living with a smoker would breathe the equivalent of smoking 1½ cigarettes.

"Policies should be based on science," Chris Coggins, the R.J. Reynolds toxicologist, said in an interview Wednesday. "I think that the (EPA) science is very, very weak."

But the industry has a long way to go toward rolling back public policy on secondhand smoke.

Public Smoking Bans

More than 600 state and local ordinances restrict smoking in public places, including Los Angeles' hotly debated restaurant ban. Across the United States, in cities large and small, a familiar sight has emerged: Smokers congregating outside. . . .

[As of September 2000 employers have a legal right to restrict smoking in the workplace or to implement a totally smoke-free workplace policy.]

In May 1994, a congressional subcommittee approved a bill, introduced by Rep. Henry A. Waxman (D-Los Angeles), that would ban smoking in most buildings, except restaurants and private clubs.

There is no smoking on domestic flights. There is no smoking in the White House. . . . There is no smoking with your Big Mac; McDonald's . . . banned tobacco in its corporate-owned restaurants. Taco Bell and Jack in the Box followed suit.

In 1993, the U.S. Supreme Court ruled in favor of a Nevada prisoner who called his cellmate's smoke cruel and unusual punishment. Custody battles have been settled by giving preference to parents who do not smoke.

The turnabout from a smoking to a smoke-free society seems to have occurred overnight. It could not have happened, anti-smoking advocates say, without science.

"Twenty years ago, I tried to have one room in a cruise ship declared smoke-free and I was told I was crazy," said John Banzhaf, a law professor at George Washington University who runs Action on Smoking and Health, or ASH. "Who at that time would have figured that 30% of all our businesses would be smoke-free today? . . . Things are moving amazingly quickly, and it is the scientific, medical underpinning that has changed the complexion of the issue."

Secondhand Smoke and Illnesses

Today, several hundred scientific studies link secondhand smoke to a variety of diseases: lung and other cancers, heart disease, respiratory infections including bronchitis and pneumonia, asthma and sudden infant death syndrome (SIDS), which claims the lives of babies as they sleep. This research is responsible for an oft-quoted statistic: About 53,000 Americans die each year from secondhand smoke.

"The evidence is so clear," says Mark Pertschuk, co-director of Americans for Non-Smokers Rights. "Everybody and his brother is lining up to ban smoking."

Yet the evidence, while compelling, is not as complete as Pertschuk suggests.

Of each year's secondhand-smoke deaths, 3,000 are attributed to lung cancer, 12,000 to other cancers and 37,000 to heart disease, according to the Coalition on Smoking OR Health, a nonprofit group formed by the American Lung Association, the American Heart Association and the American Cancer Society. The coalition also estimates that secondhand smoke accounts for 700 SIDS deaths a year.

Most scientists working outside the tobacco industry say the link between lung cancer and secondhand smoke is firmly established. But the evidence on heart disease—which accounts for nearly 70% of estimated deaths—is much newer, and not all scientists accept it. Only 14 studies have documented this link, and the federal government has not yet taken a position.

Nonetheless, public tolerance for secondhand smoke is waning.

A 1994 Gallup Poll showed 38% of Americans support a ban on smoking in restaurants—up 10% from 1991. Support for workplace smoking bans is at 32%, up eight points from 1991. The poll also found 36% of Americans believe secondhand smoke is very harmful to adults, and 42% believe it is somewhat harmful.

"The tide has turned," says Michael Eriksen, director of the Office on Smoking and Health at the U.S. Centers for Disease Control and Prevention. "I think an invisible line was crossed in terms of how the public feels about smoking."

The Tobacco Companies' Science

The tobacco industry is trying its best to persuade people to cross back over that line.

The vast majority of the research on secondhand smoke is epidemiological, meaning it traces patterns of disease and finds connections, rather than proving cause and effect. Based on those studies, scientists are just beginning to conduct animal research to learn the precise biological effects of secondhand smoke.

Tobacco industry officials vehemently dispute the epidemiology, including the EPA report. They say some study subjects give inaccurate information about how much smoke they have been exposed to, or whether they have ever smoked.

R.J. Reynolds officials also cite a recent report by the Congressional Research Service—the research branch of the Library of Congress—that characterized the EPA's data as "uncertain." Coggins, the Reynolds toxicologist, complains that the EPA failed to include . . . data that found no link between lung cancer and secondhand smoke.

"The epidemiological evidence is not sufficient to say that (secondhand smoke) poses a health risk," says Gio Batta Gori, a toxicologist and consultant for the Tobacco Institute, a trade industry group.

The EPA says nonsmokers face a 19% increase in their risk of developing lung cancer when they are exposed to secondhand smoke—a figure Gori describes as "a whiff of a risk."

> *"The [tobacco] industry has a long way to go toward rolling back public policy on secondhand smoke."*

He says that if 2.5% of the study subjects misclassified themselves, the research would be invalid.

But the EPA, which estimates that 1% of subjects misclassified themselves, sticks by its findings. EPA Administrator Carol M. Browner calls the agency's science "extensively documented" and said the R.J. Reynolds ads "will not distract the public from the real issue: that secondhand smoke poses a serious health problem."

Most independent scientists agree that secondhand smoke causes death and disease in healthy nonsmokers. It is particularly harmful to people who have underlying illnesses—asthma, heart disease, bronchitis and other respiratory conditions—that are exacerbated by cigarette fumes. But questions remain about just how much exposure will make a healthy person sick.

> *"The turnabout from a smoking to a smoke-free society seems to have occurred overnight."*

While living with or working near a heavy smoker is a serious health risk, the dangers of casual exposure are less clear.

"If you were a patron and you go out to eat, say, once a week, I think the disease risk may, in fact, be negligible," says Don Shopland, coordinator for the National Cancer Institute's Smoking and Tobacco Control program. "On the other hand, if you are a waitress and have to work in that environment eight hours a day for several years, you have a very substantial disease burden."

Still, Shopland says there is more than enough evidence to warrant smoking bans. He cites statistics showing that secondhand smoke-related lung cancer alone would kill 100 times as many people each year as asbestos. "And yet," he says, "if you find asbestos in a school, they will close the school."

Others—including Trichopoulos—say the risks of secondhand smoke are not commensurate with the public outcry. The real health danger, they say, is to the smoker.

A smoker is 20 times more likely than a nonsmoker to develop lung cancer—a 2,000% higher risk. But, depending on the study cited, someone who breathes secondhand smoke is 1.19 times to 1.4 times as likely as a nonsmoker to develop lung cancer—a 19% to 40% higher risk.

The Risk to Children

There is yet another ironic twist to the way science has shaped public policy: Most laws designed to curb exposure are directed at places where adults congregate—restaurants and offices. But research shows the biggest danger is to children, particularly those whose parents smoke at home. They need the most protection, yet get the least.

According to the CDC, secondhand smoke causes up to 300,000 cases of bronchitis and pneumonia each year in children under 18 months. It can trigger or worsen asthma attacks, and may also be responsible for up to 26,000 new cases of childhood asthma each year. The agency estimates that 9 million youngsters under 5 live in homes with smokers and are exposed to secondhand smoke almost all day.

Some studies show sudden infant death syndrome is 2½ times more likely to strike babies whose mothers smoke.

These figures have been used in education campaigns, including one by the CDC and another in California financed by Proposition 99, the anti-smoking initiative adopted in 1988. Studies show the campaigns are working; people are smoking less, and are more cautious about where they smoke.

In 1993, 27% of California smokers reported they did not smoke in their homes—up from 18.8% in 1992, according to Stanton Glantz, a UC San Francisco researcher who has done extensive work on secondhand smoke. Among smokers who lived with small children, 45% said they did not smoke at home.

And no matter what the research shows, a few simple truths remain: The vast majority of American adults—76%—are not smokers. Many are annoyed by secondhand smoke. It might not make them seriously ill, but it makes their clothes smell and their eyes water. And they are no longer afraid to demand change.

The Health Risks of Smoking Are Exaggerated

by Vic Bilson

About the author: *Vic Bilson is a Web content designer, an editor, and a professional photographer.*

Tobacco smoking has been fingered as a major cause of mortality and morbidity, responsible for an estimated 434,000 deaths per year in the United States.

But, did you know that the so much publicized 400,000+ "smoking-related" deaths in the US simply does not exist? That number is a heavily slanted, politically manipulated estimate using a computer model programmed with the assumptions of causality in synergy with the current political agenda against tobacco. It does not represent an actual bodycount. Those 400,000 smoking "victims" live longer than the rest of us!

Some claim that about 10 million people in the United States have died from causes attributed to smoking (including heart disease, emphysema, and other respiratory diseases) since the first Surgeon General's report on smoking and health in 1964 with 2 million of these deaths the result of lung cancer alone. In fact, they like to say that "Cigarette smoking is the single most preventable cause of premature death in the United States" [as stated by the Centers for Disease Control and Prevention]. They declare one in every five deaths in the United States is smoking related. Every year, smoking kills more than 276,000 men and 142,000 women.

How do they explain why non-smokers (75% of heart disease deaths) die from heart disease?

The World Health Organization (WHO) has projected that 10 million people a year will die worldwide from tobacco-related illness by the year 2025, more than triple the current toll.

"Bombarded by billions of dollars in tobacco advertising and promotion, 3,000 US teens start smoking every day. Half of those who wind up hooked for life will die a painful, early death from illnesses like lung cancer, heart disease, emphysema, and strokes". . . . as well as auto accidents, AIDS, suicide, violent crime, and home accidents. In the US, AIDS is the number one killer of African American men ages 25 and 44 and the second leading cause of death for black women of that age group. (US Department of Health and Human Services 10/28/98)

Cancer Scare

"Ninety-five percent of lung cancer deaths are due directly to cigarette smoking," according to Dr. Desmond Carney, oncologist at University College, Dublin, and secretary general of the International Association for the Study of Lung Cancer. Chemical dependency counselor, Debora J. Orrick, makes the [following] claim . . . "The consistency of results seen in numerous American and international research studies of environmental tobacco smoke lead to a certainty of more than 99.9 percent that secondhand smoke increases the risk of lung cancers in nonsmokers."

Women who smoke increase their risk of dying from lung cancer by nearly 12 times and the risk of dying from bronchitis and emphysema by more than 10 times. Between 1960 and 1990, deaths from lung cancer among women have increased by more than 400%—exceeding breast cancer deaths in the mid-1980s. The American Cancer Society predicted that 80,000 women would develop lung cancer in 2000 and 67,000 would die from it, as compared to 43,500 deaths from breast cancer.

Men who smoke increase their risk of death from lung cancer by more than 22 times and from bronchitis and emphysema by nearly 10 times. Smoking triples the risk of dying from heart disease among middle-aged men and women.

Smoking Out the Truth

70% of all cancers occur in non-smokers. The National Cancer Institute, National Institutes of Health report in the 1995 Information Please Almanac states that only 30% of all cancers are caused by smoking.

The Greeks are the heaviest tobacco users in the world and they have the lowest incidence of lung cancer. The Japanese smoke twice as much as Americans and yet have half the number of lung cancers per 100,000 people.

In truth, smoking is not a leading cause of cancer.

Lung cancer is primarily a condition developed in old age, with average age of onset age 65, according to

> *"The so much publicized 400,000+ 'smoking-related' deaths in the US simply does not exist."*

American Cancer Society literature. It's estimated more people will die of lung cancer in populations of older Americans, and where more older Americans live, there more lung cancer deaths will be estimated. More incidence of lung cancer and deaths from lung cancer are likely to occur in Florida than in any other state. That's where the highest percentage of retirees live. And that's where ACS estimates more lung cancers will occur. Lung cancer is a disease of old age, not smoking.

Philip Wiley sought at least $13.3 million in compensatory damages from six tobacco companies and two industry groups for the 1991 death of his wife. A jury in Muncie, Indiana agreed there is no proven connection between second-hand smoke and cancer and said cigarettes were not a defective product, that their makers were not negligent and the tobacco industry was not liable in the cancer death of a nonsmoking nurse exposed to secondhand smoke at a veteran's hospital. Industry attorneys pointed out that Mrs. Wiley's cancer may have had other causes and could have started in her pancreas, then spread to her lung.

Benefits of Smoking

Smoking may actually help reduce the risk of breast cancer in some women, according to a study, published in the *Journal of the National Cancer Institute*. The study found that smoking reduces by 50 percent the risk of developing breast cancer in women who have a rare genetic mutation that can lead to to the disease.

"In truth, smoking is not a leading cause of cancer."

Studies have shown evidence of an inverse relationship between smoking and the risk of contracting Alzheimer's disease or Parkinson's disease. In fact, most studies show that the more one smokes, the lower the risk level.

Scientists reported at the Society for Neuroscience annual meeting that they're encouraged they can design medications to capitalize on the benefits of nicotine without cardiovascular and other side effects. Apparently, they found that nicotine-like compounds can improve memory and might one day be used in pills to treat disorders like Alzheimer's disease.

Demographic Evidence

Smokers represented nearly 50% of the adult male/female population for several decades in the United States according to the Centers for Disease Control and Prevention. Smoking among adults decreased dramatically from 42% in 1965 to 26% in 1994. During this period, smoking among the adult male population declined from 52% to 28%; adult female smoking declined from 34% to 23%. In 1994, 48 million adults 18 years of age and older (25.3 million men, 22.7 million women) were current smokers in the United States. If nearly 50% of the population smoked, you would expect at least nearly 50% of the people who die would be smokers, if smoke has nothing to do with dying. It stands to reason we should start suspecting smoke kills smokers only when over 50% of those who die in a given year are smokers. By their own statistics, only about 20% of the deaths are smokers.

At the end of World War II, about 90 percent of the adult male population of

Britain smoked. If lung cancer takes about 20–25 years to show, as some claim, then by 1965, or 1970 at the latest, we would have seen an epidemic of truly catastrophic proportions. One in every eleven British men would have been dying of lung cancer. This simply did not happen.

There hardly appears to be the profound danger anti-smoking advocates would have us believe. As a matter of fact, it would appear you have a greater chance of dying if you're a non-smoker!

> *"Studies have shown evidence of an inverse relationship between smoking and the risk of contracting Alzheimer's disease or Parkinson's disease."*

In another look at the numbers, 38% of the people who smoke live beyond 80 years old, 50% live beyond 75, and 85% live beyond 65. This compares to 43% of non-smokers living beyond 80 years old, 50% of non-smokers live beyond 75, and 85% of non-smokers live beyond 65. The government and anti-smoking lobby can't explain this disparity, so they lie.

Misrepresentation

In a rush to cover their tracks and bad statistics, anti-smoking advocates are quickly revising their numbers to be more in line with their political ambitions. In the 1960's epidemiologists estimated that smoking killed one fourth of all regular smokers. That estimate was later raised to one third. More recently they suggest that both estimates are too low. According to scientist Richard Peto, lifelong cigarette use, particularly if begun before age 20, kills at least half of all smokers.

Americans are not experiencing the "epidemic of tobacco related disease and death" the anti-smokers claim. If that were true, why would annual death rates decrease in the U.S. as cigarette sales rates increase?

Heart Disease and Cancer

Some so-called health professionals claim that lifetime risks for lung cancer from cigarette smoking are about 10 percent and lifetime risks for obstructive pulmonary disease due to cigarettes is 30 percent. Researchers have claimed that non-smokers exposed to secondhand smoke over a long period of time exhibited a tiny but measurable increase in fatty deposits on their arterial walls and as such was responsible for some heart attacks. In fact, the arterial deposits in question are caused by diets rich in fats and cholesterol, and by lack of exercise, not secondhand smoke.

If smoking is the cause for obstructive pulmonary disease, how do you explain the incidence of these diseases in people who have never smoked and have not been exposed to secondhand smoke? The lifetime risk of cardio-pulmonary disease associated with smoking is a myth. 90% of heart disease is due directly to plaque accumulation in the arteries and the statistics that indicate smoking is responsible for 20 to 30% of these diseases is purely hypothetical.

One researcher suggested reducing overall fat intake to less than 10% (total caloric intake) would eliminate 90% of heart disease deaths (regardless of all other lifestyle factors, including smoking). Of course, his research did not go over well with milk and meat marketing boards or others with vested interest in our consumption of fat laced foods.

Nobody knows what chemicals in smoke cause cancer. Scientists have spent hundreds of millions of dollars looking for them, examining ~5,000 compounds comprising 95% of smoke by weight. Individually some are carcinogens, some are actually anti-carcinogenic, but none accounts for the effect of active smoking. . . .

So, why does the government make such a big deal about tobacco causing cancer and death when the research doesn't even support their claims? . . . It's because of money, control, and jurisdiction.

Smoking Does Not Cause Lung Cancer

by James P. Siepmann

About the author: *James P. Siepmann is a retired physician and the editor of the* Journal of Theoretics.

Yes, it is true, smoking does not cause lung cancer. It is only one of many risk factors for lung cancer. I initially was going to write an article on how the professional literature and publications misuse the language by saying "smoking causes lung cancer," but the more that I looked into how biased the literature, professional organizations, and the media are, I modified this article to one on trying to put the relationship between smoking and cancer into perspective. (No, I did not get paid off by the tobacco companies, or anything else like that.)

When the tobacco executives testified to Congress that they did not believe that smoking caused cancer, their answers were probably truthful and I agree with that statement. Now if they were asked if smoking increases the risk of getting lung cancer, then the answer based upon current evidence should be "yes." But even so, the risk of a smoker getting lung cancer is much less than anyone would suspect. Based upon what the media and anti-tobacco organizations say, one would think that if you smoke, you get lung cancer (a 100% correlation). You would at least expect a 50+% occurrence before someone used the word "cause."

Would you believe that the real number is less than 10%? Yes, a US white male (USWM) cigarette smoker has an 8% lifetime chance of dying from lung cancer but the USWM nonsmoker also has a 1% chance of dying from lung cancer. In fact, the data used is biased in the way they are collected and the actual risk for a smoker is probably less. I personally would not smoke cigarettes and take that risk, nor recommend cigarette smoking to others, but the numbers were less than I had been led to believe. I only did the data on white males because they account for the largest number of lung cancers in the US, but a similar analysis can be done for other groups using the Centers for Disease Control data.

You don't see this type of information being reported, and we hear things like, "if you smoke you will die," but when we actually look at the data, lung cancer accounts for only 2% of the annual deaths worldwide and only 3% in the US.

Smoking Risks Are Relatively Small

When we look at the data over a longer period of time, such as 50 years as we did here, the lifetime relative risk is only 8 percent. . . . That means that even using the biased data that is out there, a USWM smoker has only 8 times more risk of dying from lung cancer than a nonsmoker. It surprised me too because I had always heard numbers like 20–40 times more risk. Statistics that are understandable and make sense . . . it may be a new avenue of scientific inquiry.

The process of developing cancer is complex and multifactorial. It involves genetics, the immune system, cellular irritation, DNA alteration, dose and duration of exposure, and much more. Some of the known risk factors include genetics, asbestos exposure, sex, HIV status, vitamin deficiency, diet, pollution, shipbuilding and even just plain old being lazy. When some of these factors are combined they can have a synergistic effect, but none of these risk factors are directly and independently responsible for "causing" lung cancer!

> *"The risk of a smoker getting lung cancer is much less than anyone would suspect."*

Take a look in any dictionary and you will find something like, "anything producing an effect or result." At what level of occurrence would you feel comfortable saying that X "causes" Y? For myself and most scientists, we would require Y to occur at least 50% of the time. Yet the media would have you believe that X causes Y when it actually occurs less than 10% of the time.

Misleading Media

As ludicrous as that is, the medical and lay press is littered with such pabulum and gobbley-guk. Even as a web literate physician, it took me over 50 hours of internet time to find enough raw data to write this article. I went through thousands of abstracts and numerous articles, to only find two articles that even questioned the degree of correlation between smoking and lung cancer (British lung cancer rates do not correlate to smoking rates) and another two articles which questioned the link between second hand smoke (passive smoking) and lung cancer. Everywhere I looked the information was hidden in terms like "odds ratio," "relative risk," or "annualized mortality rate," which most doctors probably could not accurately define and interpret, let alone someone outside the medical profession. The public relies on the media to interpret this morass of data, but instead they are given politically correct and biased views.

If they would say that smoking increases the incidence of lung cancer or that smoking is a risk factor in the development of lung cancer, then I would agree. The purpose of this article is to emphasize the need for using language appropriately in the medical and scientific literature (the media as a whole may be a lost cause).

Everything in life has risk; just going to work each day has risk. Are we supposed to live our lives in bed, hiding under the blanket in case a tornado should come into our bedroom? We in science have a duty to give the public accurate information and then let them decide for themselves what risk is appropriate. To do otherwise is to subtly impose our biases on the populace.

Theoretics

We must embrace Theoretics as a discipline as it strives to bring objectivity and logic back into science. Every article/study has some bias in it, the goal is to minimize such biases and present the facts in a comprehensible and logical manner. Unfortunately, most scientists have never taken a course in logic and I'm sure that English class was not their favorite. Theoretics is a field of science which focuses on the use of logic and appropriate language in order to develop scientifically credible theories and ideas which will then have experimental implications. As someone whom I respect says, "Words mean things." Let us use language and logic appropriately in our research and the way that we communicate information.

Yes, smoking is bad for you, but so are fast-food hamburgers, driving, and so on. We must weigh the risk and benefits of the behavior both as a society and as an individual based on unbiased information. Be warned though that a society without risk shall cease to exist. Let us be logical in our endeavors and true in our pursuit of knowledge. Instead of just waiting for lung cancer to get me (because the media and a lot of the medical literature told me that smoking causes lung cancer), I can enjoy my occasional cigar even more now . . . now that I know the whole story.

The Health Risks of Secondhand Smoke Are Exaggerated

by Sara Mahler-Vossler

About the author: *Sara Mahler-Vossler has a doctorate in business and has been an associate professor of management at Hartwick College in New York.*

It's a lot easier to scare people than it is to unscare them. When guilt is added to fear, the task is even tougher. Americans have been convinced that environmental tobacco smoke, or ETS, is dangerous. Of course they're frightened, and smokers have been made to feel guilty. They fear they are hurting, maybe killing others—maybe even their own children. Media-mediated and neighbor-reinforced, this scary message about ETS gets an even wetter Pavlovian slaver when the alarm-bell ringers are top government officials or those with names followed by lots of letters and fancy affiliations. But these highly publicized claims from seemingly trustworthy sources don't hold up under close scrutiny.

"Ridiculous!" you say, "Why would our own government (or the *New York Times*) want to lie about this?" Let's look.

The Centers for Disease Control and Prevention issued a warning rivaling a surgeon general's: "Mothers who smoke 10 or more cigarettes a day actually can cause as many as 26,000 new cases of asthma among their children each year." The origins of this phantom statistic are tucked away in back sections of the Environmental Protection Agency's unreadable tome on ETS—a near guarantee that no one actually will get to it. From my reading of it, however, I detected a postmodern evolution of Darwinian selectivity. The EPA carefully picked a subset of 10 existing studies on childhood asthma and ETS to review. Then, it fished within these studies to find the shark bait.

They decided to highlight only four of the 10 to base their assessment of increased risk of childhood asthma from ETS. Then the agency completely dismissed the one study showing absolutely no effect. Next, from the numerous results contained in the remaining three studies, the EPA considered only those they liked. After cherry-picking findings from the cherry-picked subset of their cherry-picked set of studies, the EPA number crunchers pronounced it "reasonable" to use a range of 75 percent to 125 percent as their estimated increased risk for developing asthma in children whose mothers smoke 10 or more cigarettes per day. They then creatively projected this increased risk to the entire population.

Suddenly, between 8,000 to 26,000 new cases of childhood asthma could be attributable to mothers smoking 10 or more cigarettes a day, or so reads the government's report. And with another pass of the federal government's magic wand, another 26,000 new cases of childhood asthma could be seen as caused by moms who smoke half a pack.

ETS in the Workplace

Moving as if ETS were even more deadly than sarin gas, the Occupational Safety and Health Administration, or OSHA, in April 1994 proposed new regulations tantamount to a total ban on workplace smoking in the United States. For employers willing to foot the bill, the proposed rule would permit smoking areas only if "enclosed and exhausted directly to the outside, and maintained under negative pressure sufficient to contain the tobacco smoke." Additionally, no work of any kind is allowed in this smoking area. The only people permitted to enter this area to do any work would be cleaning staff.

> *"These highly publicized claims [of the dangers of ETS] from seemingly trustworthy sources don't hold up under close scrutiny."*

How did OSHA come up with a rationale for this sweeping prohibition? First, they looked at all the 13 studies with findings on occupational ETS and lung-cancer risk. From these, OSHA chose only one on which to base its estimate of increased risk from workplace ETS. OSHA's reasoning: This particular study was large and well-designed. But so were others in this group! This was the only study among the 13 with a result to OSHA's liking.

Opposed by a range of individuals and groups, OSHA's proposed rule generated more than 100,000 letters; the required public hearing lasted an unprecedented six months. The prohibition plan still seems alive and stubbornly kicking within the halls of Palace OSHA.

Smoking in the Skies

In an amazing feat of federal legerdemain, the Department of Transportation, or DOT, managed to convince the International Civil Aviation Organization (a U.N. agency) to pass a resolution that airliners should absolutely and universally prohibit smoking. DOT created its very own fat research report to reinforce its point. . . .

The technique used by DOT was to measure the amount of "bad stuff" from tobacco smoke in the cabins' air. They expected to find higher concentrations in planes with smoking sections than in those without. Since smoking bans already were enforced on domestic flights, no-smoking planes readily were available for comparison. Their state-of-the-art measurements were surprising: Once past the "boundary rows" (the first three next to the smoking section), average levels of respirable particles and carbon dioxide actually were lower on smoking flights than on no-smoking flights. Average levels of nicotine were low enough to be undetectable past the boundary rows on the majority of flights. On the minority with detectable nicotine levels, the difference, measured in micrograms (1 billionth of 2.2 pounds) per cubic meter (3 1/3 feet) of air was a minuscule 1/20 of 1 microgram. Average carbon-monoxide levels were a rousing 0.2 micrograms per cubic meter higher on smoking flights! There were, however, 200 fewer parts per million of headache-making carbon dioxide on the smoking flights than on the nonsmoking.

> *"The authors [of a study] . . . failed to find a 'statistically significant' relationship between the children's exposure to tobacco smoke and any respiratory illnesses."*

But DOT had a mission. So their crystal ball predicted over a span of 20 years, four excess lung cancer deaths among the entire U.S. cabin-crew population. Shazam! Then DOT declared that smoking should be extinguished from the skies, since it would be too expensive sufficiently to improve the ventilation and filtration of airline-cabin air. The expense, twenty dollars per flight, max, or a big 36 cents per smoker on a full Boeing 747, or 93 cents on a 727. Incidentally, smoking isn't the only reason to improve airline ventilation.

ETS and Kids

Publicity about a recent study on ETS and acute or chronic respiratory illnesses in children admonishes, "Children exposed to tobacco smoke . . . suffer over 10 million days of restricted activities . . . 21 percent more than unexposed kids." Ten million is a catchy, scary number, but where does it come from? The study appeared in the May 13–18, 1996, issue of the "scientific" journal, *Tobacco Control*, the very title of which should raise questions about scientific objectivity. The authors show right up front that they failed to find a "statistically significant" relationship between the children's exposure to tobacco smoke and any respiratory illnesses.

But then they reported that the parents in their sample were asked how many days the children missed school or had their activities restricted. Somehow, the researchers "found" here the relationship they wanted—albeit small. No attempt was made to determine if other factors could account for this, nor was there any attempt to account for the contradiction.

The authors took their preferred finding, extrapolated it to the whole U.S. population and, eureka!, 10 million. Note: This number signifies only that, for unknown reasons, parents who smoked recalled keeping their kids home slightly more than parents who didn't, but it doesn't mean that the smokers' offspring were sicker. The researchers did not publicize the fact that the number of childhood illnesses linked to ETS exposure was negligible. This is misleading reporting.

ETS and Heart Disease

If the prohibitionists could make a convincing case that ETS causes heart disease (the leading killer in the United States) in nonsmokers, they'd be in clover. Even with a small excess risk from ETS, really big death estimates could balloon. The lack of hard evidence doesn't stop tobacco prohibitionists and their scientific allies from trying. Witness a front-page story in the *New York Times* on May 20, 1997: A team of Harvard researchers released the results of a 10-year study which claimed that regular exposure to other people's smoke at home or at work almost doubled the risk of heart disease. Case closed? Not according to Steve Milloy, executive director of The Advancement of Sound Science Coalition, who called the study another case of "epidemiologists trying to pass off junk science as Nobel prize work."

A day after the Harvard report was issued Milloy issued the following statement: "The new study uses statistics—not science—to claim that secondhand smoke increases the risk of heart attack by 91 percent. This abuse of statistics is such a problem that the National Cancer Institute issued a press release in 1994 advising that increases in risk of less than 100 percent were not to be trusted. And for good reason. In the new study, there was no measurement of even one person's exposure to secondhand smoke. The researchers relied on unverified questionnaires. Also, it is likely the researchers did not adequately consider other competing causes for heart disease such as smoking, lack of exercise, poor diet and so forth."

Is there a pattern here? An Aug. 15, 1996, Associated Press bulletin claimed that the results of a huge study showed that never-smokers married to smokers had about a 20 percent higher risk of dying from heart disease than with nonsmoking mates. Actually, this result only applied to the never-smoking men married to current smokers. No excess risk was found for never-smoking women married to current smokers. Oops! They forgot to mention that part of it. And wouldn't there be more heart disease in the husbands of heavy smokers than of light smokers if, in fact, ETS exposure had something to do with it? But in this study, the finding was upside-down; the more the wife smoked, the lower the husband's risk. Hmmm!

> *"No excess risk [for heart disease] was found for never-smoking women married to current smokers."*

Smoking

This piece of information also failed to appear in the AP story.

Since the 1960s, our government, aided by an assortment of do-gooders, has been trying to get everyone to quit smoking. It started out reasonably by disseminating information that smoking was linked to some nasty diseases. Having our best interests at heart, concerned professionals and government officials apparently felt compelled to devise stronger arguments to make us do the right thing. The government funded research in order to confirm the idea that ETS is harmful. But, the research results came in mostly indeterminate and, in some cases, negative. What to do? Well, since it's for a good cause, ignore the reality. Claim lots of dire findings. Divide, scare and hector.

The Health Risks of Cigar Smoking Are Exaggerated

by Jacob Sullum

About the author: *Jacob Sullum is the senior editor of* Reason *magazine, a monthly publication of politics and culture.*

A television ad sponsored by the California Department of Health Services shows a young man in a dark suit holding a cigar while sitting in a big leather chair. "Say, Chad," the narrator asks him, "any idea how many cigarettes you'd need to equal the nicotine in that big fat stogie?"

After Chad repeatedly guesses wrong, the narrator says, "No, Chad, you'd have to smoke more than 70." Seventy cigarettes appear in poor Chad's mouth as a slogan is displayed at the bottom of the screen: "CIGARS. The Big New Trend in Cancer."

When the Chad ad was first aired, the *Los Angeles Times* described it as "comparing the effects of one cigar to smoking the equivalent of 70 cigarettes." According to the *Sacramento Bee*, "the television spot . . . points out that smoking cigars poses the same health risks as smoking cigarettes."

False Advertising

Those are fair interpretations of the ad's implicit message. The problem is, the message isn't true. It is well established by decades of research that cigar smokers face hazards far less serious than cigarette smokers do, primarily because they inhale less smoke. That point was confirmed by a National Cancer Institute (NCI) report that was wrongly portrayed as equating the risks of cigars and cigarettes.

Even in terms of nicotine delivery, the California ad is misleading. First, there is little evidence that nicotine contributes to smoking-related diseases (which is why pharmaceutical companies can sell nicotine gum and patches as safe alternatives to cigarettes). Second, a cigar that delivered the amount of nicotine in three and half packs of cigarettes would be very unusual. According to the NCI report, a premium cigar typically yields about as much nicotine as a dozen cigarettes, not 70.

The Chad ad is part of a nationwide strategy aimed at scaring people away from cigars. U.S. cigar consumption rose more than 50 percent from 1993 to 1997, with imports of premium cigars more than quadrupling. Just when tobacco's opponents thought that smoking was permanently declasse, cigars have become newly fashionable among the rich and famous. In response, public-health officials and anti-smoking activists are calling for federal warning labels, restrictions on advertising and promotion, and regulation by the Food and Drug Administration (FDA). Meanwhile, they have been encouraging the press and the public to believe that cigars are just as dangerous as cigarettes, if not more so.

The implied equation between cigars and cigarettes was conspicuous in late February 1999, when the Department of Health and Human Services (HHS) released a report recommending government warnings on cigars "analogous to the labels on cigarettes." Most cigar packages already carry a warning that "this product contains/produces chemicals known . . . to cause cancer, and birth defects or other reproductive harm." Making the case for additional warnings, surgeon general David Satcher declared that "cigars contain the same kind of carcinogens that are found in cigarettes, and in some cases, maybe more of them." While this is true as far as it goes, it does not mean that the typical cigar smoker absorbs the same dose of carcinogens or faces the same cancer risk as the typical cigarette smoker. Satcher also said, "The absence of labels implies cigars are different and don't carry the same risk." (They are, and they don't.) Predictably, the Associated Press reporter got the impression that, as she put it in her lead, "scientists say [cigars] are just as deadly as cigarettes."

Misunderstandings

Satcher is not the only official whose pronouncements about cigars are easily misinterpreted. Consider how Michael Eriksen, director of the Office on Smoking and Health at the U.S. Centers for Disease Control and Prevention (CDC), described the hazards of cigars in a May 1997 *New York Times* story: "Tobacco is tobacco is tobacco." Asked to interpret that quote, CDC epidemiologist Ann Malarcher says, "There are a lot of meanings to that." The literal meaning, of course, is a tautology; but surely many people would understand Eriksen to be saying that all tobacco products are equally hazardous. The *Times* itself went further, announcing that cigars pose "higher risks than . . . cigarettes."

"Cigar smokers face hazards far less serious than cigarette smokers do, primarily because they inhale less smoke."

We could simply blame journalists for leaping to the wrong conclusions, but it's clear that public-health officials are giving them a good shove. In February

1998, for example, the NCI's Donald Shopland told *USA Today*, "You're smoking a whole pack of cigarettes" when you smoke a cigar. And Jack Henningfield, an addiction specialist who contributed to the NCI's cigar report, told the *Wall Street Journal*, "It will help explode some of the myths about cigars," including the belief "that they are relatively safe."

Yet when it came out in April 1999, the NCI monograph demonstrated, once again, that cigars are safer than cigarettes. Overall, the NCI reported, daily cigar smokers get oral and esophageal cancers almost as often as cigarette smokers. But they face much lower risks of lung cancer, coronary heart disease, and chronic obstructive pulmonary disease—the three main smoking-related causes of death. The upshot can be seen in mortality figures. In a 1985 American Cancer Society study cited by the NCI, men who smoked a cigar or two a day were only 2 percent more likely to die during a 12-year period than nonsmokers, a difference that was not statistically significant. By contrast, the mortality rate was 69 percent higher for men who smoked a pack of cigarettes a day.

The only really bad news for cigar smokers in the NCI report applied to a small minority. The NCI emphasized that the risk from cigars increases with the frequency of smoking and the degree of inhalation. Cigar smokers who inhale deeply face measurably higher risks of heart disease and emphysema (though still not as high as those faced by cigarette smokers), and the risk of lung cancer for a five-cigar-a-day smoker who inhales approaches the

> *"[Cigar smokers] face much lower risks of lung cancer, coronary heart disease, and chronic obstructive pulmonary disease."*

risk for a pack-a-day cigarette smoker. That sort of cigar smoker is quite unusual, however. "As many as three-quarters of cigar smokers smoke only occasionally," the NCI noted, and "the majority of cigar smokers do not inhale." Since the available data apply only to people who smoke at least one cigar a day, "the health risks of occasional cigar smokers . . . are not known."

Moderation Is Key

In other words, there is no evidence that smoking cigars in moderation—with moderation defined by the way most cigar smokers actually behave—poses a measurable health risk. But because the NCI emphasized that "cigars are not safe alternatives to cigarettes" (something no one had claimed), this point was lost on the press. The headline in the *San Francisco Chronicle* read, "Cancer Institute's Warning on Cigars: Just As Bad As Cigarettes." An Associated Press story said the NCI report was "intended to equate dangers posed by the two products." The article began, "Smoking cigars can be just as deadly as smoking cigarettes." This is like saying that riding a bicycle "can be just as deadly" as riding a motorcycle. It's true in the sense that both activities can result in fatal accidents. But that does not mean they are equally dangerous.

After the NCI report came out, John Banzhaf, executive director of Action on Smoking and Health, said FDA regulation of cigars was all the more vital "now that we know that cigars are as dangerous as cigarettes." Banzhaf also filed a petition with the Federal Trade Commission (FTC), asking it to require "cigarette-like warnings on cigar labels and in ads." FTC chairman Robert Pitofsky seemed sympathetic to the idea. "If the National Cancer Institute is saying that regular cigar smoking is roughly as

> *"Public-health officials should recognize that misleading comparisons between cigars and cigarettes have the potential to backfire."*

dangerous as cigarette smoking," he told the *Washington Post*, "I would expect people would want health warnings."

Even if they do not value truth for its own sake, public-health officials should recognize that misleading comparisons between cigars and cigarettes have the potential to backfire. After seeing the California ad equating one cigar with 70 cigarettes, for example, a guy who smokes a couple of cigars a week might mistakenly conclude that he would be no worse off smoking a pack of cigarettes a day. And anyone who realizes how deceptive the ad is will probably be more inclined to dismiss other warnings from public-health agencies.

Despite such risks, we may soon be seeing more messages of this kind. In its February 1999 report, HHS called for a national "public awareness campaign about the health effects of cigars." With any luck, Chad will still be available.

Nicotine May Not Be Addictive

by Richard J. DeGrandpre

About the author: *Richard J. DeGrandpre is an independent scholar of drugs and culture and a visiting assistant professor of psychology at Saint Michael's College in Vermont.*

During the 1996 presidential election campaign, Bill Clinton successfully cast Big Tobacco as a national enemy, with Bob Dole playing the role of collaborator by downplaying the addictiveness of nicotine. Meanwhile, the Food and Drug Administration has been asserting jurisdiction over cigarettes as "nicotine delivery devices," arguing that tobacco companies intend to hook their customers, just like schoolyard drug pushers. Hundreds of pending lawsuits, including class actions and cases filed by state governments, similarly allege a conspiracy to addict smokers. These developments represent important changes in our attitudes toward cigarettes. Though justified in the name of public health, the increasing emphasis on the enslaving power of nicotine may only make matters worse.

Understanding why requires careful consideration of the conventional wisdom about tobacco addiction, which recycles mistaken assumptions about illicit drugs. During the latter half of the twentieth century, the classical model of addiction, derived from observations of narcotic abuse, increasingly has been used to describe the cigarette habit. The classical model states that consumption of certain chemicals causes a physical dependence, either immediately or after prolonged use, characterized by withdrawal symptoms—symptoms that can be avoided or escaped only by further drug use. As Steven Hyman, director of the National Institute of Mental Health (NIMH), opined recently in *Science*, "Repeated doses of addictive drugs—opiates, cocaine, and amphetamines—cause drug dependence and, afterward, withdrawal."

This cyclical model, in which the drug serves as both problem and solution, offers a simple, easy-to-grasp account of the addiction process, giving the con-

From "What's the Hook?" by Richard J. DeGrandpre, *Reason*, January 1997, vol. 28, no. 8, p. 47. Copyright © 1997 by Reason Magazine, 3415 S. Sepulveda Blvd., Suite 400, Los Angeles, CA 90034, www.reason.com. Reprinted with permission.

cept great staying power in the public imagination. In the case of smoking, this view of addiction is central to the rationale for regulating tobacco and the concern that the cigarette companies have been doping their products with extra nicotine. But the classical model tends to conceal rather than elucidate the ultimate sources of addiction, and it is just as ill-suited to the cigarette habit as it has always been for understanding illicit drug use.

Not Everyone Becomes Addicted

If a chemical compound can be addictive in the manner described by NIMH Director Hyman, we would expect anyone who regularly uses such a substance to become addicted. Yet only a minority of those who use illicit drugs—whether marijuana, cocaine, or heroin—ever develop a dependence on them. The prevalence of addiction, as defined by the American Psychiatric Association's *Diagnostic and Statistical Manual*, among users of alcohol and cocaine runs about 15 percent and 17 percent, respectively. Even in a sample of 79 regular crack users, Patricia Erickson and her colleagues at Toronto's Addiction Research Foundation found that only about 37 percent used the drug heavily (more than 100 times in their lives), and 67 percent had not used in the past month. A similar pattern holds for tobacco. In the 1994 National Household Survey on Drug Abuse, 73 percent of respondents reported smoking cigarettes at some time, but only about 29 percent reported smoking in the previous month, and not necessarily on a daily basis. Writing in the May/June *Mother Jones*, Jeffrey Klein manages to argue that nicotine enslaves its users and, at the same time, that Tobacco Inc. seeks to recruit young smokers to replace the 1.3 million Americans who quit each year. If nicotine is so relentlessly addictive, how can it be that 50 percent of all Americans who have ever smoked no longer do?

The classical model also suggests that the cigarette habit should be highly amenable to nicotine replacement therapy, such as the nicotine patch. Yet few of the tens of thousands of patch users have actually broken the habit (only about 10 percent to 15 percent succeed). In direct conflict with the classical model, most keep smoking while on the patch, continuing to consume the carcinogens in cigarette smoke while obtaining considerably higher blood levels of nicotine. A 1992 study of nicotine replacement therapy reported in the journal *Psychopharmacology* concluded that the "overall lack of effect [of the patch] on cigarette consumption is perhaps surprising and suggests that in regular smokers the lighting up of a cigarette

> *"The increasing emphasis on the enslaving power of nicotine may only make matters worse."*

is generally triggered by cues other than low plasma nicotine levels."

Most people who successfully quit smoking do so only after several failed attempts. If addiction is driven by physical dependence on a chemical—in this case, nicotine—relapse should occur during withdrawal, which for nicotine typically lasts a few weeks. Yet a sizable proportion of relapses occur long after the smoker has suffered through nicotine withdrawal. In fact, studies do not even show a relationship between the severity of withdrawal and the likelihood of relapse. As any former smoker could tell you, ex-smokers crave cigarettes at certain times and in certain situations for months, even years, after quitting. In these cases, the desire to smoke is triggered by environmental cues, not by withdrawal symptoms. This is one reason why people who overcome addiction to illicit substances such as heroin or cocaine often say they had more difficulty breaking the cigarette habit. Because regular tobacco users smoke in a wide array of circumstances (when bored, after eating, when driving) and settings (home, work, car), the cues that elicit the urge are more ubiquitous than for illicit drug use.

Nicotine Addiction or Cigarette Addiction

These failures of the classical model illustrate how conventional wisdom oversimplifies the dynamics of cigarette smoking. This reductionist view is dangerous because it ignores the psychosocial factors that underlie addiction. In coming to terms with cigarette addiction as a psychosocial process, rather than a simple pharmacological one, we need to distinguish between cigarette addiction and nicotine addiction. Certainly no one (except perhaps the tobacco companies) denies that cigarette smoking can be addictive, if by addiction one means a stubborn urge to keep smoking. But it is quite a different matter to say that nicotine accounts for the

> *"A sizable proportion of relapses occur long after the smoker has suffered through nicotine withdrawal."*

addictiveness of smoking. Nicotine withdrawal notwithstanding, nicotine alone is insufficient, and may even be unnecessary, to create cigarette addiction.

This claim can be clarified by two dramatic case studies reported in the *British Journal of Addiction* in 1973 and 1989. The earlier article described a 47-year-old woman with a two-and-a-half-year-long dependence on water, one of several such cases noted by the author. The woman reported a nagging withdrawal symptom—a dry, salty taste in her mouth—that was alleviated by the persistent drinking of water (up to 60 glasses per day). This case of dependence on a nonpsychoactive substance contrasts sharply with the second account, which described an 80-year-old woman who used cocaine without incident for 55 years. The authors reported that "she denies any feelings of euphoria or increased energy after [snorting] the cocaine nor any depression or craving for cocaine when her supplies run out. . . . She appears to have suffered no ill effects from the prolonged use of cocaine in physical, psychological or social terms." So we see that not every addiction involves drug use and not every instance of drug use involves an addiction.

To say that cigarette addiction is a psychosocial process means that social, cultural, and economic factors play a crucial role in acquiring and keeping a cigarette habit. In fact, the tendency to reduce the cigarette experience to chemical servitude may be one of the most powerful cultural factors driving addiction.

Cigarette lore wrongly teaches smokers (and smokers-to-be) that they will suffer badly if they attempt to quit, while at the same time freeing them of responsibility for their drug use once they begin. Such beliefs also

> *"Nicotine alone is insufficient, and may even be unnecessary, to create cigarette addiction."*

help romanticize cigarette smoking, elevating nicotine to a sublime abstraction. This not only reinforces the forbidden fruit effect, it helps transform the habit of smoking into a cult behavior. Smoking thus acquires the kind of meaning that the youth of America are most in search of: social meaning. As Richard Klein writes in *Cigarettes Are Sublime*, "smoking cigarettes is not only a physical act but a discursive one—a wordless but eloquent form of expression."

To counteract the forces that give momentum to drug use, the public meaning of addiction needs to be broadened to include the many, changing facets of the psychosocial realm in which we develop. "Putting people back in charge" of their addictions, as John Leo puts it in *U.S. News & World Report*, will not work if we focus only on the naked individual. Rather than pushing the pendulum of public policy between scapegoating the substance and scapegoating the individual, we should seek a middle ground. Realizing that the addiction process has at least three levels of complexity is a good place to start.

The Three Levels of Addiction

First, at the basic and most immediate level, are the short- and long-term biological processes that underlie the psychological experiences of drug use and drug abstinence. Even with the same drug, these experiences vary greatly across individuals. Scientists and journalists too easily forget that every psychological process is built on biology. Discoveries of biological mechanisms and processes underlying addiction are not proof that the problem is biological rather than social and psychological. Eating rich foods has powerful biological effects in both the short and long run, but we should not therefore conclude that the rise in obesity in the United States is a biological problem. Indeed, attempts to alter the addiction process that emphasize biochemistry (such as the nicotine patch) have met with little success.

At the next level are psychological processes (social, motivational, learning) that, although rooted in biology, are shaped by personal experience. Because each of us has unique life experiences, we do not necessarily interpret the same events in the same way. The reasons for one individual's addiction may be altogether different from the reasons for another's. . . . Still, intervention at this level has had some success with users of alcohol or illicit drugs, and several research and treatment institutions are examining methods for "matching" addicts with different treatment strategies based on their social and psychological characteristics.

Drug effects and drug addiction also vary greatly across time and place, implicating cultural factors as the third and most general aspect of drug addiction. These factors are rooted in but not reducible to psychological processes, just as psychological processes are not reducible to biology. Patterns of alcohol use around the world, which show that the prevalence of drinking problems cannot be predicted by consumption alone, illustrate the importance of culture. Italians, for example, historically have consumed large quantities of alcohol with relatively low rates of drunkenness and alcoholism. The effects of alcohol on human behavior—violence, boorishness, gregariousness—also have been shown to vary dramatically across cultures.

Given the cultural role in addiction and the radical changes that have occurred in attitudes about smoking, it is quite possible that the young smokers of today are not at all like the smokers of 50 years ago. Those who begin smoking now do so with the belief that it is addictive, causes poor health (and wrinkles!), and can be deadly. If individuals are willing to start smoking despite such knowledge, it is likely that they will acquire and keep the habit, seeming to confirm the current, politically correct image of addiction. And if this self-fulfilling prophecy is realized, chances are that interventions aimed at the social realm will continue to miss their target and fail to curtail addiction.

The Health Consequences of Smoking Are Irreversible

by Paul H. Brodish

About the author: *Paul H. Brodish is an Outcomes Research Specialist with PPD Pharmaco, Inc., a contract research organization.*

Cigarettes damage the body—gradually and insidiously—in a number of different ways. Over the years, the American Council on Science and Health and others have documented the effects. Our purpose here is to address the following key questions:

- Does a cigarette smoker who quits return to the health profile of a nonsmoker? If so, when?
- If the smoker's profile does not fully return to that of presmoking days, what effects are irreversible—and when do they become irreversible?
- What damage can be reversed—and to what extent?

One popular argument the scientific community often makes to encourage smokers to quit stems from the conjecture that all of the health effects of smoking are reversible shortly after cessation, regardless of the duration or intensity of the smoking exposure. Unfortunately, this conjecture is not true. Teenagers, in particular, may be overly complacent about smoking because they believe—incorrectly—that they can smoke for a few years and then quit without suffering any long-term effects. This complacency is especially troubling in light of the recent finding, reported by the Centers for Disease Control and Prevention (CDC), that teen smoking rates have increased by nearly a third within the last six years.

Teen smokers who believe that all the health hazards of cigarettes will disappear in a puff of smoke when they quit—who assume that smoking from, say, age 16 to age 28 will have no long-term effects—often fall back on an "I can always quit tomorrow" (or next month or next year) philosophy. They trust—mistakenly—that any adverse health consequences they may incur during their smoking years will disappear when, eventually, they stop lighting up. But another recent study has reported that the quitting success rate among teenagers is very low: Less than 16 percent of the 633 teen smokers in the study were able to kick the habit. This report will summarize the data on this vital—but rarely covered—topic. . . .

Cigarettes and Public Health

Cigarette smoking is the leading cause of preventable death in the United States. It accounts for almost 500,000 deaths per year, or one in every five deaths. Cigarette smoking contributes to a remarkable number of diseases, including coronary heart disease, stroke, chronic obstructive pulmonary disease, peripheral vascular disease, peptic ulcer disease, and many types of cancer. Of the 46 million smokers in the United States, 34 percent try to quit each year—but less than 10 percent succeed.

According to the CDC, approximately 80 percent of current adult smokers began smoking before their 18th birthday. Each day over 3,000 teenagers light up for the first time. Most teens are aware of smoking's hazards, but few are worried about them. Moreover, most teen smokers quickly become addicted to nicotine: They report that they want to quit but are unable to do so. And teen smokers experience high relapse rates and debilitating withdrawal symptoms.

The bottom line is that smoking is costly, both to individual smokers and to society as a whole: Recent long-term studies indicate that about half of all regular cigarette smokers will eventually die from their addiction.

With smoking, the reversibility of health effects is influenced by many factors. Among those factors are smoking exposure (the number of cigarettes per day and the duration of smoking) and physiologic susceptibility. The presence of other diseases, genetic variables, and even nutritional factors also enter into susceptibility assessment. Quitting brings benefits at any age, but there are "threshold" amounts of smoking that irreversibly increase the risk for some diseases.

The good news is that quitting prolongs life and reduces the risk of tobacco-related cancers, myocardial infarction, cerebrovascular disease, and chronic obstructive pulmonary disease (COPD). Current knowledge of the irreversible effects of smoking, organized by organ systems, follows.

Respiratory System

Smoking directly irritates and damages the respiratory tract. Each year a one-pack-a-day smoker smears the equivalent of a cup of tar over his or her respiratory tract. This irritation and damage cause a variety of symptoms, including bad breath, cough, sputum production, wheezing, and respiratory infections such as bronchitis and pneumonia. These effects can be reduced, but not entirely reversed, by quitting.

Smoking is the principal risk factor for developing COPD—i.e., chronic bronchitis and emphysema. Emphysema is characterized by permanent structural changes in the lung tissue. The deterioration in lung function associated with

COPD is directly related to duration of smoking and the number of cigarettes smoked ("pack-years"). Smoking during childhood not only increases the risk of developing COPD in adulthood but also lowers the age of its onset.

Cigarette smoking during childhood and adolescence increases the number and severity of respiratory illnesses. It also causes retardation in the rate of lung development and in the level of maximum lung function—and retardation in lung growth during childhood means that the lungs may never attain normal function and development.

Everyone—smoker and nonsmoker alike—experiences a slow decline in lung function starting at about age 30. In smokers this gradual decline starts both from a lower baseline and at an earlier age. Smokers suffer from decreased lung reserve: They are unable to run—or even walk—as far or as fast as their peers who have never smoked. Smokers thus can expect permanently impaired lung function relative to their nonsmoking peers.

Irreversible Lung Damage

With sustained abstinence from smoking, the rate of decline in pulmonary function among smokers returns to normal; but lung reserve remains decreased relative to those who have never smoked. Quitting improves pulmonary function by about 5 percent within a few months of cessation, and COPD mortality rates decline among quitters versus continuing smokers. A recent study in more than 10,000 boys and girls aged 10 to 18 confirmed that cigarette smoking is associated with mild airway obstruction and slowed growth of lung function. The study, which covered a period of 15 years, also demonstrated that girls are more susceptible than boys to smoking's adverse effects on the growth of lung function.

Smoking-induced chronic irritation of the respiratory lining and the wide variety of carcinogens in cigarette smoke induce permanent changes in the cells lining the respiratory tract. These changes can lead to cancer. Cigarette smoking is, in fact, the major cause of lung cancers of all major histologic types.

During the past half century, lung cancer rates have dramatically increased in women, to the extent that lung cancer is now the leading cause of cancer death in women, exceeding both breast cancer and colon cancer. (Smoking has, of course, been the leading cause of cancer death in men

> *"Teenagers . . . believe—incorrectly—that they can smoke for a few years and then quit without suffering any long-term effects."*

for decades.) This increased female mortality parallels the increase in cigarette smoking among women.

Smoking cessation reduces lung cancer risk by 30 percent to 50 percent 10 years after quitting, and the risk continues to decline with further abstinence. The risk in ex-smokers always remains increased compared to that in nonsmokers, however. It is now known that almost 50 percent of all lung cancers are diagnosed in ex-smokers, and this finding is not surprising in view of the fact that there exist a "plethora of studies demonstrating a lag between smoking initiation and increased incidence of lung cancer of several decades," according to Professor Jonathan Fielding.

One recent study noted that 75 percent of ex-smokers showed changes in their DNA indicative of precancerous lesions, as compared to only 3 percent of people who had never smoked. At the May 1998 meeting of

> *"The bottom line is that smoking is costly, both to individual smokers and to society as a whole."*

the American Lung Association, data were presented showing that former smokers continued to develop lung cancer at rates 11 to 33 times higher than nonsmokers. The data also showed that the shorter the time since quitting, the higher was the ex-smoker's risk. Increased risk was still noted in former smokers after more than 20 years of abstinence, however.

Heart and Circulation

Premature coronary heart disease (CHD) is one of the most important medical consequences of smoking. Smoking acts both independently of and synergistically with other major risk factors for heart disease. Sadly, sudden death may be the first sign of CHD—and sudden death is four times more likely to occur in young male cigarette smokers than in nonsmokers. Women who use both cigarettes and oral contraceptives increase their risk of developing CHD tenfold. The excess risk of coronary heart disease is halved in quitters (as compared to continuing smokers) one year after cessation, but the risk level doesn't return to that of nonsmokers until 15 years after quitting.

In a recent study of atherosclerosis, the progression of fatty deposits in the carotid artery was found to be dependent on total pack-years of tobacco exposure, rather than on the patient's current smoking status. This finding indicates that atherosclerosis progression may also be cumulative and irreversible, at least after some degree of baseline exposure.

Cerebrovascular accident (CVA), or stroke, causes brain damage that usually leaves its victims with permanent disabilities. Smokers' excess risk for stroke appears to return to that of nonsmokers within 5 to 15 years of cessation. One recent study suggests, however, that an ex-smoker's risk remains high for at least 20 years after cessation. In addition, it was recently learned that the incidence of "silent strokes"—events that are harbingers of both severe strokes and dementia—is increased in anyone who has ever smoked.

Finally, smoking is a strong risk factor for several types of blood-vessel disease. Smoking causes poor circulation to the legs by narrowing the blood vessels that supply these extremities. Quitting reduces, but does not eliminate, this risk. Once it becomes symptomatic, such circulatory impairment often requires surgical intervention.

Eyes and Mouth

Two recent studies published in the *Journal of the American Medical Association* tracked 50,000 smokers for approximately 12 years. The studies found a two- to threefold increased rate among both smokers and ex-smokers of developing macular degeneration, an irreversible form of blindness. The risk was significant even among those who had quit smoking 15 or more years earlier. Researchers speculate that smoking causes vision loss by restricting blood flow to the eye.

Cataracts (clouding of the lens) are another visual problem associated with cigarette smoking. A recent study showed a 40-percent higher rate of cataracts among 3,600 people who had ever smoked, as compared to nonsmokers.

Cigarette smoke irritates the eyes, nose, throat, and gums. These tissues respond by thickening and by undergoing cellular changes that can eventually lead to mouth, throat, or esophageal cancer. Gum disease and tooth loss are also common among smokers. Quitting halves the risk for cancers of the oral cavity and esophagus during the first five years after cessation, but ex-smokers always have an increased risk as compared to the risk in those who have never smoked.

Cigarette-smoke irritants can also permanently damage the tissues of the larynx. The effect of this is a noticeable deepening and hoarseness in the voices of chronic smokers. Quitting reduces the risk of developing laryngeal cancer. Vocal-cord polyps (noncancerous growths) are also strongly related to tobacco exposure, and such polyps rarely disappear without surgery.

Smoking causes bladder and kidney cancer. It is, in fact, the strongest risk factor known for developing bladder cancer. An ex-smoker's risk of bladder cancer is reduced by one half within a few years after quitting, but a higher risk of developing these cancers remains for decades.

Digestive Organs and the Musculoskeletal System

Smoking decreases esophageal sphincter pressure. The decrease in pressure allows acid to reflux from the stomach into the esophagus. This can lead to esophagitis and to permanent esophageal stricture (or narrowing).

Smoking is also a risk factor for pancreatic cancer and colon cancer. The risk of pancreatic cancer is somewhat reduced 10 years after quitting; ex-smokers remain at higher risk indefinitely, however. The relationship between cigarette smoking and colon cancer has only recently become clearer. Two large, prospective American studies have detected such a relationship, but a recent Swedish study detected no such relationship in smokers observed for 20 years. The American researchers felt that it might take as long as 35 years for the colon cancers secondary to smoking to appear: In a study that looked at a large group of people who had smoked for as few as 10 years, the American researchers detected progressively more severe colonic lesions with increasing time after quitting.

Smoking is associated with osteoporosis (thinning of the bones due to loss of bone minerals) in women, and with spinal disk disease in both sexes. Lost bone calcium cannot be fully recovered, and degenerative bony changes are irreversible. Osteoporosis predisposes to fractures and is responsible for much disability, especially in elderly women. A recent meta-analysis of 29 studies involving almost 4,000 hip fractures concluded that one of every eight fractures was attributable to smoking, although the rate was lower for ex-smokers than for current smokers.

Reproduction

Infertility is more common among smokers but is not irreversible. The damage done to smokers' babies during pregnancy often is irreversible, however. Smoking during pregnancy is associated with dire consequences for the baby as a fetus, as a newborn, and even as a child. Recognition of the evidence of this damage has prompted researchers to designate it as "fetal tobacco syndrome."

Miscarriage is two to three times more common in smokers, as are stillbirth due to fetal oxygen deprivation and placental abnormalities induced by the carbon monoxide and nicotine in cigarette smoke. Smokers have a fourfold risk of having a low birthweight baby; such babies are more likely than normal-weight babies to have impaired physical, emotional, and intellectual development. The authors of a 1996 study found that women who smoked

> *"Cigarette smoking is . . . the major cause of lung cancers of all major histologic types."*

during pregnancy were 50 percent more likely to have a child with mental retardation of unknown cause than were nonsmoking women.

Sudden infant death syndrome is significantly associated with smoking, as is impaired lung function at birth. Women who quit smoking as late as the first trimester may diminish some of these risks, but the risk of certain congenital malformations—such as cleft palate—is increased even in women who quit early in pregnancy.

Smoking causes premature facial wrinkling through vasoconstriction of the capillaries of the face (vasoconstriction decreases the flow of oxygen and nutrients to facial skin cells). The effect of this reduced blood flow is visible in deep crow's feet radiating from the corners of the eyes and pale, grayish, wrinkled skin on the cheeks. These effects may emerge after as few as five years of smoking and are largely irreversible, except through costly and traumatic facial surgery.

Permanent Damage

There should be no illusions as to the dangers of cigarettes. The combination of a highly addictive, pharmacologically active substance—nicotine—and an array of noxious chemicals cunningly packaged in a highly efficient delivery mechanism can permanently and drastically affect health.

People who smoke for as brief a period as 10 years show a substantially higher rate of death, disease, and disability. Risks to the respiratory system, especially, and risks of cancer continue to plague the ex-smoker for years after quitting. Smokers should not delude themselves that they can smoke safely for 10 to 15 years and then—if they are among the lucky few who *can* quit—become as healthy and risk-free as if they had never smoked at all. . . .

In summary, the following irreversible health effects have been proven to be associated with smoking:

- Retardation in the rate of lung development and lung function—i.e., decreased lung reserve—in childhood and adolescent smokers, as well as a markedly increased risk of developing COPD.
- Cancer risk: 75 percent of ex-smokers show DNA changes suggestive of tumor development; 50 percent or more of lung cancers are now being diagnosed in ex-smokers.
- Circulatory impairment to the heart, brain, and legs.
- Visual impairment and loss.
- Vocal-cord polyps (growths) and hoarseness.
- Bone mineral loss (osteoporosis), hip fractures, and spinal arthritis.
- Serious health consequences for children born to smoking mothers.
- Premature facial wrinkling and graying of the skin after as few as five years of smoking.

This report is intended for everyone—smokers, never-smokers, and ex-smokers alike—but it is aimed particularly at those who have not yet become addicted to tobacco. To everyone we say, Remember: Only 20 percent of smokers who try to quit are successful on a long-term basis; for four out of five of those who take up smoking, the very decision to begin is itself irreversible.

Secondhand Smoke Is Harmful

by Melanie Scheller

About the author: *Melanie Scheller is a contributing editor at* Current Health *2, a publication dedicated to improving the knowledge of nutrition, health, and fitness among teenagers.*

If you're in a smoking environment at home or work, your health could be at risk. Here's why.

"How can I get my mother to realize that her smoking is bad for my asthma?"

The student who posted that cry for help on a popular Web site has a reason to be concerned. Studies have shown that breathing someone else's cigarette smoke increases the number and severity of asthma attacks. But if your mom—or anyone you know—is one of the estimated 48 million adults in the United States who smoke, finding room to breathe isn't always easy.

Coping with "secondhand smoke" can be a complicated business. Whether the smoker is your mom or the man next to you in a restaurant, it's hard to find a tactful way to say, "You're making me sick. Please stop smoking." You'll improve your chance of success if you have a firm grasp of the facts.

Where There's Smoke . . .

Secondhand smoke (also known as environmental tobacco smoke [or ETS]) is composed of "mainstream smoke," which is exhaled by the smoker, and "sidestream smoke," which is given off by a burning cigarette, pipe, or cigar between puffs. When former Surgeon General Luther Terry published the first report on the hazards of smoking to smokers in 1964, it seemed logical to assume that cigarette smoke was equally hazardous to nonsmokers. But it took years to confirm this through research.

In 1986 the National Research Council of the National Academy of Sciences produced a groundbreaking report on the health effects of environmental tobacco smoke. After reviewing the evidence, the Council concluded that secondhand smoke was responsible for 3,000 deaths from lung cancer each year in the United States.

Since then, the connection between secondhand smoke and lung cancer has grown steadily. One study found that "passive smoking" raises a non-smoker's chance of getting lung cancer by 26 percent. In 1992, the United States Environmental Protection Agency classified secondhand smoke as a Group A carcinogen, the category reserved for the most dangerous cancer-causing substances. Secondhand smoke contains more than 4,000 chemicals, at least 40 of which are suspected to cause cancer.

> *"Breathing someone else's cigarette smoke increases the number and severity of asthma attacks."*

Behind the Smokescreen

Lung cancer isn't the only deadly effect of secondhand smoke. The American Heart Association (AHA) estimates 40,000 die each year from heart and blood-vessel disease caused by secondhand smoke. The risk of heart disease increases by up to 30 percent among those exposed to secondhand smoke at home or at work, according to the AHA. The American Cancer Society reports that heart, lung, and other diseases caused by secondhand smoke result in 53,000 deaths annually. It is the third-leading cause of death in the U.S., after smoking and alcohol.

Like many hazardous materials, secondhand smoke has its greatest impact on infants and children. The authors of a 1997 report in the medical journal *Archives of Pediatric and Adolescent Medicine* stated, "More children are killed by parental smoking than all unintentional injuries combined."

Secondhand smoke can be deadly to infants. Sudden infant death syndrome, or SIDS is the major cause of death in the United States in infants between the ages of 1 month and 1 year. Infants whose mothers smoked during and after pregnancy are three times more likely to die of SIDS than infants of non-smoking mothers.

Secondhand smoke also causes many serious health problems. It contributes to as many as 300,000 cases of pneumonia, bronchitis, and other respiratory infections in infants and children every year. It is also one of the risk factors in the development of childhood asthma, causing 8,000 to 26,000 new cases each year. And it has been found to increase the number of middle ear infections in children whose parents smoke.

Clearing the Air

Even if you choose not to smoke, you can easily become an "involuntary smoker." In a 1998 survey done by the AHA, 47.7 percent of nonsmoking, working adults 17 years and older reported that they are exposed to secondhand smoke at home or at work. Another study by the AHA, May 1998, reported secondhand smoke depletes the body's stores of antioxidants, which act as a natural defense against heart disease.

The good news is that change is in the air. Many employers and businesses have become smoke-free, while local governments have banned smoking in public buildings and other facilities. Also, new products and techniques are available to help smokers who want to quit.

If you smoke, one of the best things you can do for yourself and the people you care about is to stop smoking. If you don't smoke, one of the best things you can do for yourself and the smokers you care about is to help them stop smoking. Then we'll all be able to breathe more easily.

Cigar Smoking Is Dangerous to Human Health

by Jim Motavelli

About the author: *Jim Motavelli is the editor of* E/The Environmental Maga-*zine, a publication dedicated to educating people about the environment and encouraging its preservation.*

Demi Moore wants to light up your life. "There's something about smoking a cigar that feels like a celebration," says the star, a *Cigar Aficionado* cover celebrity. "It's like a fine wine. There's a quality, a workmanship, a passion that goes into the making of a fine cigar."

That equation—fine cigar equals fine wine—has firmly taken hold among the pretentious neo-yuppies who love the "naughty," politically incorrect frisson that comes with every public puff. No longer is the cigar smoker stereotyped as the heartless capitalist depicted in a *Working Assets* ad; now he—and increasingly, she—is cool, a rebel with a rich inner life. The tattoo and the belly-button ring of the late 90s, and its indulgence is catered to by upscale cigar bars with walk-in humidors. Americans smoked an incredible 4.5 billion cigars in 1996, a 44.5 percent rise from 1993.

Cigar Chic

Stogie smokers have their own version of *Playboy*. Portly publisher Marvin Shanken, who first went after "connoisseurs" with the magazine *Wine Spectator*, launched *Cigar Aficionado* in 1992 as the quarterly everyone thought would crash and die after the first issue. Instead, it became a rare publishing success story, growing immensely to its current status as a bimonthly with 400,000 subscribers and page after page of high-end advertising. "It's really a lifestyle magazine for men, most of whom are quite affluent," says Niki Singer, a senior vice president. "The country was ready for it. Our readers have been told to moderate their drinking, to abstain from eating red meat—they're tired of being dictated to. They're adults, and smoking cigars is their choice."

If letters to the editor are any clue, *Cigar Aficionado*'s readers are guided largely by seething resentment to assaults on their white male privilege. "On one side is individual freedom and pleasure," writes Michael Washington through teeth clenched around a Romeo y Julieta. "On the other side is everybody who seems to know what's best for me."

Like any collector hobby, cigar "nonconformists" have their holy grail—in this case, it's the forbidden fruit of banned Cohibas and Hoyo Epicures from Cuba. The U.S. Customs Service seized 96,216 Cuban cigars in 1,400 incidents during 1996. Though they display no evident affection for Fidel Castro, cigar fanatics seem to have no qualms about bolstering his regime by dealing in smuggled goods or making special appearances. Ardent anti-communist Arnold Schwarzenegger was reportedly on hand at the 30th anniversary of the Cohiba in Havana in February 1999, defying the travel ban to Cuba along with fellow stars Danny DeVito and Jack Nicholson.

A Costly Indulgence

All this would be merely amusing if cigars weren't a serious health threat. But despite the fact that many cigar smokers don't inhale and indulge their passion only occasionally, there's clear and mounting evidence that—even without a printed warning on the package—cigars are hazardous to your health (and to the health of people forced to breathe in secondary smoke).

According to the American Lung Association (ALA), health studies show that men who smoke five or more cigars per day are two to three times more likely to die of lung cancer than are nonsmokers. Cigar smokers also face higher death rates from chronic obstructive pulmonary disease, and are particularly at risk from laryngeal, oral and esophagal cancers (death rates equal those of cigarette smokers, according to the American Cancer Society). The *American Journal of Public Health* adds that cigar smokers are more likely than nonsmokers to suffer from persistent coughs and phlegm buildups, and have a greater likelihood of contracting peptic ulcers. A study of 25,000 Swedish men found that cigar smokers were five times more likely to die from an aortic aneurysm (the result of a weakened blood vessel) than nonsmokers.

The U.S. Centers for Disease Control and Prevention (CDC) reports that an autopsy study of lungs from

> *"Americans smoked an incredible 4.5 billion cigars in 1996, a 44.5 percent rise from 1993."*

1,443 men found that 53.5 percent of the cigar smokers were in some stage of emphysema. A single large cigar can contain as much tobacco as a whole pack of cigarettes, and smoking just two or three a day results in that level of exposure to nicotine (which, along with tar, is heavily concentrated in cigars). Even holding an unlit cigar in your mouth is dangerous, as it may enable nicotine absorption. Secondary smoke is also an issue. "Because cigar smokers do not fully inhale a majority of the smoke when they light up," says Thomas Gibson, ALA president, "they deposit more secondhand smoke in the air around them." This secondhand smoke contains some 4,000 chemicals, 23 of which are poisonous and 43 of which are carcinogenic.

"When you see glamorous individuals like Arnold Schwarzenegger and Bill Clinton smoking cigars, what you're not seeing is the health effects," says Ann Malarcher, an epidemiologist in the CDC's Office on Smoking and Health. "It's almost like it's considered a safe habit, and really for many of the oral cancers, it's just as deadly as cigarette smoking." In a 1998 issue, *Barron's* magazine warned investors that the cigar fad was about to burst—largely because of forthcoming health studies.

Starting 'Em Young—and Female

Though cigars are, like cigarettes, an "adults-only" product whose sale to minors under 18 is prohibited, the law hasn't had much practical effect. Illegal sales of cigars to young people reportedly exceed cigarette sales. The CDC, working with the Robert Wood Johnson Foundation, released a study in May 1997 revealing that some 27 percent of high school students admit to having smoked a cigar in the previous year. In two New York counties, 13 percent of ninth-grade students said they had smoked a cigar in

> *"It's almost like it's considered a safe habit, and really for many of the oral cancers, it's just as deadly as cigarette smoking."*

the last 30 days. "We're shocked by the magnitude of cigar smoking among high school students," says Michael Erisken, director of the CDC Office on Smoking and Health. "It's clearly an outgrowth of the glamorization of cigar smoking among adults."

The Washington-based Action on Smoking and Health (ASH) filed a petition with the Food and Drug Administration (FDA) asking that it assert regulatory authority over cigars. "Their argument has been that they don't regulate cigars because they're not as attractive to kids," says ASH Executive Director John Banzhaf. "But the CDC study shows an absolutely alarming rise in teenage cigar smoking. Our feeling is that every regulation that applies to cigarettes, including restrictions on promotion and advertising, should also apply to cigars." Dr. Anne Davis, a pulmonary physician in New York and a past president of the American Lung Association, agrees with Banzhaf. "Cigars certainly should be regulated," she says. "I would tell any teenager thinking of taking up the habit that cigars can be as addicting as cigarettes, and that while you may not feel the effects now, you could down the line."

Thanks to "glamorous" smokers like Demi Moore and Madonna, cigar smoking has also caught on among women. Although the industry trade association estimates that only four percent of cigar smokers are women, gender health statistics are already being affected. Dr. Nieca Goldberg, the head of cardiac rehabilitation at Lenox Hill Hospital in New York, points out that "the leading cancer in women is not breast cancer anymore—it's lung cancer, because of the increase in smoking among women."

> *"The leading cancer in women is not breast cancer anymore—it's lung cancer, because of the increase in smoking among women."*

Norman Sharp, president of the Washington-based Cigar Association of America, after first proclaiming that his organization "doesn't get into" health matters, downplayed the CDC data by pointing out that it found only 2.6 percent of teenagers smoking 50 or more cigars a year. "To be a teen is to experiment," he says. "Our industry's experience is that kids don't smoke cigars." Really? A letter in the winter 1996 issue of *Cigar Aficionado*: "I began smoking cigars in high school and have grown to become a true aficionado." A second letter, same magazine: "I admit my first indulgence was before the proper age of 18 years, feeding my rebellious attitude."

"I'm not rich," says aquarium cleaner and cigar smoker Bryan Gallagher of Huntington, Long Island, puffing away at a recent restaurant cigar night. "But smoking a cigar makes you feel like you're in the upper echelon," hobnobbing with the likes of Schwarzenegger and DeVito.

Nicotine Is Addictive

by the *Harvard Mental Health Letter*

About the author: *The* Harvard Mental Health Letter *is a monthly publication of the Harvard Medical School Health Publications Group.*

By now everyone knows that nicotine is addictive, and only tobacco salesmen deny it. Cigarette smoking and other forms of tobacco use fit the reasonable definition of substance dependence (another term for addiction) given in the American Psychiatric Association's (APA's) diagnostic manual. The symptoms include tolerance (a need to increase the dose to achieve the desired effect), using the drug to relieve withdrawal symptoms, unsuccessful efforts or a persistent unfulfilled desire to cut down on the drug or stop using it, and continued use of the drug despite knowing of its harm to yourself or others. Although nicotine dependence is usually not thought of as a psychiatric disorder, the APA classifies it as one, along with alcoholism and other serious drug addictions.

Spokesmen for the tobacco industry, using their own special definitions, prefer to say that their product is merely "habituating." If they are correct, and nicotine is not addictive, then nothing is. About 45 million people in the United States smoke cigarettes, cigars, or pipes, and a few million use snuff or chewing tobacco. More than half of smokers light their first cigarette within a half hour of waking up, and 30% have never stopped smoking for as long as a week. Most of them wish they had never taken up the habit. Fifty million others have managed to quit, but it is not easy. Only 5% succeed on the first attempt, and only a third hold out for as long as two days on each try. Forty percent have tried three times or more. A third try to stop each year, but only 3% to 5% of them remain abstinent for as long as a year. Relapse is rare after that, but in one study 20% still felt cravings five to ten years later. Habitual heavy users of heroin and cocaine say it is easier to give up those drugs than to stop smoking. The average age for taking up the habit has dropped from 20 in 1910 to 15 in 1997. About half of adolescents who smoke two or more cigarettes develop an addiction, and three-fourths of them try to quit at least once before they graduate from high school.

Experimental animals will not inject nicotine as enthusiastically as, say, cocaine, but in existing social conditions it is easier for human beings to become and remain dependent on tobacco. Compared to other drugs, cigarettes are inexpensive and easily available. They can be used at almost any time because they do not noticeably or uncomfortably interfere with perception, body movements, thinking, or speech. Tolerance to any unpleasant effect develops quickly, and once a certain level is reached, there is no further tendency to increase the dose. Until recently, tobacco addiction had little effect on a person's work or social life. The rewards of smoking are immediate, the penalties long delayed.

The Road to Addiction

The tobacco cigarette is a highly effective drug delivery device: the nicotine goes straight to the lungs, where it is absorbed by oxygenated blood, sent to the heart, and pumped into the arteries and the brain. The nicotine in snuff and chewing tobacco, which is absorbed mainly through the mucous membranes of the mouth, reaches the brain more slowly, but constant use maintains a steady level in the blood and brain.

Some signs of nicotine dependence are smoking at least a pack a day, smoking when sick in bed, having to light the first cigarette soon after waking up, smoking more often in the morning, and wanting to smoke in forbidden places such as movie theaters and airplanes. The withdrawal reaction, which begins within hours, consists of craving, irritability, anxiety, restlessness, and increased appetite. The symptoms are milder if withdrawal is gradual, and most of them fade in a few days, but the craving may persist for months or even years, stimulated by cues associated with smoking—persons, places, situations, and sensations, including the sight of cigarettes and the smell and taste of tobacco.

The biological basis of this addiction is the action of nicotine at a certain type of receptor for the neuro-transmitter acetylcholine. The resulting increase in the numbers and sensitivity of nicotinic receptors probably accounts for the withdrawal reaction. These receptors stimulate the release of another neuro-transmitter, dopamine, in the brain's reward or motivation center, which is located in the nucleus accumbens, part of the limbic region. It is the same nerve circuit activated by cocaine and amphetamines, which enhance the effects of dopamine more directly. Experimental animals are most likely to use a drug compulsively when doses are delivered rapidly and intermittently and consistently accompanied by

> *"Most [smokers] wish they had never taken up the habit."*

other distinct sensations or actions—exactly what happens when tobacco is smoked or heroin injected.

Nevertheless, about 10% of smokers are not addicted. They smoke as much as they want and no more, usually less than half a pack a day, and they have no withdrawal symptoms. The capacity to use nicotine without addiction runs in families, and studies comparing identical with fraternal twins suggest that it has genetic roots, with a heritability (the proportion of individual differences attributable to heredity) of about 50%. Nonaddicted smokers absorb nicotine just as well as addicts, and their personalities are no different. Their immunity to addiction may depend partly on the kinds, numbers, and sensitivity of nicotinic receptors in their brains, a characteristic that does not depend on heredity alone. There is some evidence, for example, that all other things being equal, the children of mothers who smoke during pregnancy are more likely than average to become smokers; their brains may have been affected by prenatal exposure to nicotine.

> *"The withdrawal reaction . . . consists of craving, irritability, anxiety, restlessness, and increased appetite."*

Like any drug dependency, nicotine addiction is also influenced by the price, availability, and social acceptability of the drug. Since the 1960s, the proportion of smokers in the American population has fallen from 41% to 26%. The trend is weakening in the '90s, and has always been strongest among people with high income and education (today only 15% of American college graduates smoke). Tobacco consumption in underdeveloped countries has increased greatly in the last 20 years. Here and elsewhere, the poor are more likely to continue smoking because they have lower expectations of life, less sense of control over the future, less access to information, and less opportunity for treatment.

Mental Disorders and Alcoholism

Others at high risk for nicotine dependence are people with psychiatric disorders, especially depression, alcoholism, and schizophrenia. The authoritative Epidemiologic Catchment Area (ECA) survey suggests that in the United States, about 70% of men and 80% of women with a history of major (severe) depression are or have been tobacco addicts. In demographic or social groups that for other reasons have a low proportion of smokers, a high proportion of the remaining smokers are likely to be depressed. Among American female college graduates, for example, nearly half of the smokers have suffered or are now suffering seriously from depression.

Sometimes depression leads to nicotine dependence. Even smoking that starts before clear depressive symptoms appear may be self-medication for early mood changes. But the main reason for the connection is probably an underlying predisposition to both depression and smoking. A high rate of either major depression or nicotine dependence in a family predicts a high rate of the other. Twin studies suggest that the heritability of the association is 60%.

Nicotine addicts who have suffered from depression also find it more difficult to quit. The ECA survey found that 33% of smokers with a history of depression had succeeded in quitting, as compared with 50% of those who had no psychiatric diagnosis. Statistically, women have a harder time quitting than men—a difference that is probably explained by the higher rate of depression in women, since men and women without a history of depression quit at the same rate. Only smokers who have been depressed in the past tend to become depressed when they stop, and this effect is independent of the severity of their withdrawal symptoms. Occasionally someone who successfully quits has to be advised to take up the habit again when it proves to be the only way to lift a severe depression.

More than 75% of schizophrenic patients smoke, most of them heavily. Since smoking usually begins at about the age when schizophrenic symptoms first appear, they could be medicating themselves. Nicotine may be improving their concentration, counteracting their emotional unresponsiveness, or relieving some of the side effects of antipsychotic drugs. (Many schizophrenic patients take medications that may block nicotinic receptors.) A more likely reason for the association is a common vulnerability, possibly with a genetic basis. Schizophrenic patients may suffer from a malfunction in the brain's filtering mechanisms that is partially or temporarily corrected by smoking. They are deficient in the response called sensory gating, which prevents overstimulation and the resulting confusion. Most people are less easily startled by a loud noise if they have heard a similar but softer sound a fraction of a second earlier; schizophrenic patients are more likely to be unaffected by the warning. According to some recent research, they show an improvement in this response immediately after smoking.

"The poor are more likely to continue smoking because they have lower expectations of life, . . . less access to information, and less opportunity for treatment."

As implied by the familiar image of a man with a cigarette in one hand and a glass of beer or whiskey in the other, smoking is also associated with the use and abuse of alcohol and other drugs. Most people who become dependent on alcohol, cocaine, or heroin are tobacco addicts first. In this respect, as in others, alcoholism may be the male equivalent of depression in women: 25% of male college graduates in the United States who are or have been smokers also are or have been alcoholics. The vast majority of patients admitted to residential treatment programs for alcoholism and other addictions are smokers, and in the long run tobacco is the most lethal of their drug habits. There is evidence that this association between different kinds of drug dependence has genetic roots. Interestingly, nonaddicted as well as addicted smokers have a higher than average rate of alcoholism and drug dependence.

Health Hazards

The reasons for quitting are familiar but worth restating. Tobacco accounts for about one in seven deaths in the United States—one in three between the ages of 35 and 70. At a pack a day, an estimated four years of life is lost; at two packs a day, eight years. Only 5% of men alive at age 85 have been smokers all their lives.

The products of burning tobacco irritate the body's airways and clog the lungs with mucus that damages the walls of the alveoli (air sacs). The resulting chronic bronchitis and emphysema claim many lives. Substances in cigarette smoke, especially benz[a]pyrene and nitrosamines, are the main cause of lung cancer, which kills 8% of men and 4% of women in the United States. The rate of lung cancer in pipe and cigar smokers is lower but still high. All tobacco users are susceptible to cancers of the lip, tongue, throat, cheek, and upper respiratory tract, as well as cancer of the esophagus, cervix, and bladder.

> *"Tobacco accounts for about one in seven deaths in the United States."*

Heart disease is an even greater danger. Components of tobacco smoke raise blood pressure, promote clotting, reduce the heart's oxygen supply, and damage the walls of arteries, eventually causing arteriosclerosis. People who smoke a pack a day have three times the average rate of coronary artery disease. The risk increases proportionately with the number of cigarettes smoked; it falls 50% in the first year after quitting and comes down to average 10 years later. Smoking also causes strokes and peripheral vascular disease (mainly in the leg arteries). Carbon monoxide, a common product of incomplete burning, probably raises the risk to the heart by reducing the oxygen-carrying capacity of the bloodstream.

Women who smoke during pregnancy have a high rate of miscarriages and difficult births. Their babies are smaller than average, more likely to develop asthma and other respiratory diseases, and less likely to survive. They may also suffer from slightly delayed development and a higher rate of attention deficit disorder, although it is not clear whether their mothers' smoking is the cause of these problems rather than a sign of a family vulnerability.

People who spend time in the presence of smokers absorb some of the products themselves. The material in secondhand or sidestream smoke is burned less completely, producing proportionally more contaminants than mainstream smoke in smaller particles which may work their way more deeply into the lungs. According to some estimates, secondhand smoke accounts for several thousand lung cancer deaths each year in nonsmokers. Others doubt that the amount involved is sufficient to affect health except in unusual circumstances—say, spending most of the day in a small room with a smoker. But no one denies that passive smoking can be annoying and uncomfortable, especially for people who have not developed a tolerance to the smell, throat irritation, and respiratory effects.

Pros and Cons of Nicotine

Nicotine itself is one of the less dangerous components of tobacco smoke. It can be lethal when absorbed through the skin accidentally in large quantities in the form of spilled insecticide. Certain South American Indian healers deliberately take dangerously high doses to produce a hallucinatory trance state in which they communicate with spirits. But it is doubtful whether the nicotine in ordinary cigarettes is a serious health risk. It is not carcinogenic. In theory, it may contribute to cardiovascular disease by raising the heart rate and blood pressure, causing abnormal heart rhythms, altering the movement of artery walls, or lowering the ratio of high-density to low-density cholesterol. But there is slight evidence of harm at the doses usually taken. In an experiment reported in 1996, rats were forced to inhale air loaded with nicotine 20 hours a day, five days a week, for two years—most of a lifetime. Despite blood levels of nicotine twice as high as a heavy human smoker's, their lungs, hearts, and arteries were not damaged, and their longevity was normal. It remains to be seen whether this result can be extrapolated to judge the effects of nicotine on human beings, with their much longer lives.

Nicotine may even have some beneficial effects. It keeps weight down by inhibiting the appetite and slightly increasing the body's metabolic rate during active periods. Smokers have a low risk of Parkinson's disease, which is caused by a dopamine deficiency; nicotine may supply some protection by causing the release of dopamine. (On the other hand, low dopamine activity may reduce the desire to smoke in people with incipient Parkinson's disease.) The effects of nicotine on mood and performance, as tested in many experiments, are limited and variable. It apparently eases simple repetitive tasks but has little effect on complex thinking and problem-solving. A half dozen drugs are already known that block or activate one or another of the nicotinic receptors. Researchers are seeking artificial compounds that act at some of those locations and may enhance mood or performance without the risk of addiction.

"Natural Tobacco" Products Pose Serious Health Risks

by the American Lung Association of California

About the author: *The American Lung Association works to prevent lung disease and promote lung health through education, community service, advocacy, and research.*

Do not be fooled by "natural tobacco" products that are marketed to teens and college students. They're not healthier. In fact, natural tobacco can be deadlier than average cigarettes.

Unfortunately, for today's youth and young adults, forms of natural tobacco, including bidis, clove cigarettes, cigars, chew/dip tobacco, pipe tobacco and organic cigarettes, are viewed as trendy and perhaps even healthier, despite the real health risks.

"Natural tobacco doesn't have anything to do with being healthier," says Ross Payson, project director for tobacco programs at the Dental Health Foundation. "Natural means it has a small percentage of non-synthetic substances. It's a marketing scam."

Natural tobacco often contains higher concentrations of tar and nicotine, and the smoke has greater levels of toxic agents such as carbon monoxide, hydrogen cyanide, ammonia and carcinogenic hydrocarbons. This not only increases the smoker's risk of developing lung cancer or other diseases, but it also jeopardizes the health of everyone in the room.

"You're still inhaling carbon monoxide and 400 carcinogens and poisons," Payson says.

American Lung Associations in California and other groups, including the Dental Health Foundation and the California Youth Advocacy Network, are implementing new programs and adjusting others to combat the rise in natural tobacco use by teens and college students, and the ultimate disease and premature death it will cause.

Bidis

A recent report released by the Centers for Disease Control and Prevention (CDC) found in a Boston-area study of 642 high school students that 40 percent had tried bidis and 16 percent were current bidi smokers.

"Natural tobacco is an up and coming issue," says Jennifer Williams, director of Tobacco Control for the American Lung Association of the Central Coast. "We found that older and younger teens are asking about bidis and cloves because they think they are a lot safer than cigarettes."

Bidi cigarettes, also known as beadies or beedies, are handrolled tendu leaves containing low-grade tobacco and tied up with string. Widely available in grocery stores and convenience stores for about half the cost of cigarettes, the paper-wrapped bundles of bidis come in several flavors including cinnamon, vanilla and strawberry.

Nearly 70 percent of bidi brands do not have warning labels as required by law, according to a Dental Health Foundation fact sheet.

Bidis are known as the "poor man's cigarette" in India. They are made by women and children in India's poor households, according to research compiled by the Dental Health Foundation. In addition to a lack of health precautions and poor working conditions, it has been shown that bidi assemblers absorb nicotine through their skin.

"Teens are aware of the health risks from smoking tobacco and it may not have an impact," Payson says. "But I think it would have more of an impact if they knew that children in India roll 1,000 to 1,500 bidis a day, for 30 cents per day in a 12- to 16-hour work day. They work under poor conditions and there is no quality assurance."

Fighting a Dangerous Trend

To combat this dangerous rise in bidi smoking, American Lung Associations throughout the state are implementing Teens Against Tobacco Use (TATU), in cooperation with the American Heart Association and the American Cancer Society. The all-day training and education workshop trains teens how to talk to children about the dangers and myths about tobacco.

"We found that using teens as anti-tobacco educators for elementary school children is more effective than using adults," Williams says.

More than 90 percent of adult smokers started smoking in their teens, resulting in the creation of tobacco control programs that focus on early prevention in junior high and high school. There are very few prevention and cessation programs for young adults ages 18 to 25.

> *"Natural tobacco can be deadlier than average cigarettes."*

"Mind the Gap" is an advocacy project implemented by the American Lung Association of Santa Clara-San Benito Counties focusing on college students in that age category on seven college campuses in Santa Clara and San Benito counties in California. The project focuses on education and prevention.

"Our goal is to make campuses smoke-free," says Francis Capili, project director at the American Lung Association of Santa Clara-San Benito Counties. "We want to protect people from secondhand smoke and limit tobacco accessibility."

Tobacco Companies Target Colleges

"Some tobacco companies are targeting colleges by sponsoring fraternity parties and giving away free chew tobacco," says Susan Snoke, college project consultant for the California Youth Advocacy Network.

Snoke is part of a three-year project to develop student advocacy coalitions at California schools, including the University of California at Davis, University of California at Santa Cruz, Sonoma State University, San Diego State University and Vanguard University of Southern California.

The coalitions are implemented and facilitated by college students who determine which campus smoking policies and issues to address. Marie Boman, a college liaison for anti-tobacco advocacy at San Diego State University (SDSU), led a movement to enforce SDSU's no smoking policy in a specific campus building. She was able to get the college to remove cement ashtrays from the breezeways and the doorways to prevent smoke from flowing inside the building.

Boman volunteers for the American Lung Association and believes tobacco companies are currently targeting colleges for cigars, clove cigarettes and chew/dip tobacco.

"There's a misconception in defining cloves as natural," Boman says. "Clove cigarettes are processed just like regular cigarettes." Clove cigarettes are typically made of 60 percent poor quality tobacco. They deliver twice as much nicotine, tar and carbon monoxide as tobacco cigarettes in addition to the unknown hazards associated with chemicals in cloves. Clove cigarette smokers can suffer immediate effects including coughing up blood, nose bleeds, severe sore throats, and upper respiratory infections.

Cigar Smokers More Likely to Develop Cancer

Although cigars may also be marketed as a natural and safer alternative to cigarettes, they contain larger amounts of nicotine and carcinogens. A bill requiring cigar manufacturers to add labels comparing the danger of cigar smoking with cigarettes or warning smokers of cancer and other diseases was passed by the state Legislature in September 1999.

"It seems that cigars are also being pushed on college campuses to the 18- to 24-year-old men and women," Payson says. "Cigars are marketed to portray cigar smokers as affluent, powerful and sexy."

Cigar smokers are four to 10 times more likely than non-smokers to die of cancer of the mouth and throat. Cigarettes can contain 11 milligrams of nicotine while a cigar can contain as much as 444 milligrams. Cigars also give off five times as much tar and 25 times more carbon monoxide than a cigarette.

So even cigar smokers who say they don't inhale are risking their health. Not only are they choking on their own secondhand smoke, along with everyone else in the room, cigar smokers suffer higher rates of cancer and other diseases.

"Smoking is smoking is smoking," Payson says. "Tobacco, no matter the form, is poisonous and addictive to all ages."

Chapter 2

Does Advertising by Tobacco Companies Influence People to Smoke?

Chapter Preface

For decades, cigarettes were advertised like any other product. However, in 1970, in response to a 1964 report by the surgeon general on the health risks of smoking, Congress passed a ban on cigarette advertisements on television and the radio. Recently, antismoking activists have attempted to take Congress's action a step further by seeking a complete ban on advertising by tobacco companies.

In November 1998, such figures as R.J. Reynolds's Joe Camel and Philip Morris's Marlboro Man were banned from tobacco advertising campaigns because antitobacco activists claimed that human and cartoon figures in advertisements targeted children and encouraged them to smoke. The rugged cowboy image of the Marlboro Man and the suave Joe Camel appealed to youth with their emphasis on independence, rebellion, and freedom, according to the antitobacco lobby. As stated by the World Health Organization, "Children around the world are surrounded by advertisements portraying tobacco use as fun, sophisticated, modern and Western. . . . Tobacco advertising exploits the vulnerabilities of youth by offering tobacco as the means to a positive self-image and as the key to acceptance by their peers. Advertising also sends the message that smoking is an 'adult' behaviour, and offers cigarettes as a badge of independence and maturity." Supporters maintain that the tobacco companies strive to maintain their clientele by using such advertising techniques to recruit young smokers to replace the thousands of customers lost each year to smoking-related illnesses.

Tobacco companies argue that their advertising only aims to influence brand choice among confirmed smokers and does not influence people to smoke. According to the Tobacco Manufacturers' Association, "Cigarette advertising promotes competition by bringing the availability of brands to the attention of the smoker. . . . Manufacturers advertise to: reinforce brand values and sales to existing smokers to support their continued choice; invite smokers of competitive brands to switch; introduce existing smokers to new brands and new developments in the market. . . . There is no convincing evidence that advertising causes anybody—adult or child—to start smoking."

In the following chapter, authors debate whether advertising influences people to smoke.

Tobacco Ads Manipulate People into Smoking

by James R. Rosenfield

About the author: *James R. Rosenfield is a leading speaker and writer on marketing and direct marketing practices.*

Cigarette advertising seems to say everything—but the truth.

Looking at cigarette advertising these days is like staring into the abyss. You get a vertiginous sense of queasy fascination. Tobacco hucksters seem to be whistling past the graveyard, throwing caution to the winds as they do startling high-risk takes on health, death, and transgression.

It's as if R.J. Reynolds [RJR], in giving up the cuddly and studly Joe Camel, has decided to abandon symbolism completely and go for in-your-face bathroom humor and sexual innuendo. Billboards combine death and anality in a dark pun that Freud would have loved: "Kiss Your Additives Goodbye." Other billboards feature the slogan "No bull." That's the Winston campaign, which pins the tail of a "healthier," all-natural cigarette right smack on the donkey of death.

How about post–Joe Camels? Joe's phallic nose is a picture of maidenly restraint compared to a two-page magazine spread that features a bare-chested, belt-loosened, underwear-displaying young fellow fleeing a shotgun-wielding farmer, the latter's sheet-clad daughter displayed in a window, curled up in bed smoking a clearly post-coital Camel. Thumbing its nose at authority figures like the Surgeon General, the headline "VIEWER DISCRETION ADVISED" tells us that "THIS AD CONTAINS: SS Satisfied Smoking . . . FV Farm Violence . . . AN Animal Nudity." Regarding the latter, the backside of a chicken maintains the anal theme so directly communicated by the Winston folks.

Now in postmodern, post-Monica [Lewinsky] America, taste is long dead, anything goes and infantilism has become a prevailing mode. It's part of the barbaric decadence of these fin de siecle United States. Nonetheless, this smirky, cocky, arrogant approach clearly works best with young people; the younger the better.

From "Cigarettes Are Good for You! And—They're Not Addictive!" by James R. Rosenfield, *Direct Marketing*, November 1998. Copyright © 1998 by Rosenfield and Associates. Reprinted with permission.

Cigarettes Are Good for You!

It's almost a relief to look at the elegant, cagey, and subversive mailing pieces that seem to constitute the bulk of Brown & Williamson's marketing communications. . . .

No transgressive death flirtations here, and not even a hint of RJR's clumsily self-referential irony. Nope, Brown & Williamson falls back on the oldest cigarette marketing trick in the book in a campaign for Capri: Cigarettes are good for you.

They can't come out and say it, of course, the way Luckies did, in those antediluvian days when they were "recommended by more doctors than any other brand." But they sure can imply it, and they sure do.

"Soothe away stress" suggests the outer envelope, "Relax, Refresh, Retreat" promises a beautifully designed booklet. "With Capri, enter a world of serenity, harmony and contentment with Aromatherapy and Capri Superslims."

"Your free guide to the Art of Aromatherapy is enclosed right here. Indulge yourself in the wonders of Aromatherapy, anytime, right in your own home. A soothing facial sauna, relaxing massage with pure essential oil or a luxuriating scented bath. Here's all you need to know to free yourself from everyday cares."

"Enter a private world all your own with these aromatherapy hints" headlines a folder, inside which four handsome slips of paper tell various aromatherapy stories. To give you a flavor or better, a scent (and the mailing package, by the way, is indeed scented):

"Herbal Extract, Fragrance of Energy . . . Herbs, such as rosemary, sage, and thyme, have been the life-enhancing alchemy of every human culture since the beginning of recorded history. Throughout the ages, priests, doctors, and shamans from China to the Americas brewed aromatic potions from herbs to relieve mental, physical and emotional illness and discomfort. . .

"Aromatherapists use rosemary as a general tonic to boost flagging energy and spirits. Inhaling the essence of rosemary in steaming water seems to lessen . . . headaches."

Double Duplicity

There are two levels of subversion going on here.

The first level is pretty obvious: By focusing on something "therapeutic," Brown & Williamson suggest concern about your health and well-being, and anyone concerned about your well-being wouldn't sell you stuff that can kill you, right? Implication: Cigarettes are good for you, which nicely subverts reality itself.

The second level is a little subtler. Aromatherapy is part of the alternative medicine culture, and alternative medicine tends to be ideologically opposed to the conventional medical establishment. And it's the conventional medical establishment, led by the Surgeon General, that has mounted the charge against tobacco. This nets out to an implied discrediting of conventional medicine and all its works, including the Surgeon General's Warning that appears underneath a beautiful photo of a bowl of herbs.

Feminine Appeal

Another mailing piece shows a relaxed, robe-clad woman, sitting on a balcony, Tuscan rooftops in the background. Create the secrets of the world's greatest spas . . . with ingredients right from your own home.

"Capri presents your escape from everyday cares, with soothing spa recipes. From the book HOME SPA RECIPES AND TECHNIQUES TO RESTORE AND REFRESH . . ."

Two elegant cards provide instructions for "SKIN-SOFTENING MILK BATH . . . TONER . . . APPLE-OATMEAL SCRUB . . . PEPPERMINT OIL FOOT RUB."

This package is dynamically similar to the first one, subtly implying that smoking is good for you. It lacks, however, the amazing anti-medical diabolism of its predecessor.

> *"Tobacco hucksters seem to be whistling past the graveyard, throwing caution to the winds as they do startling high-risk takes on health, death, and transgression."*

Both packages contain coupons and brief questionnaires. Package one has three coupons of descending value: $3.00, $2,00, $1.00. The second one has three coupons, all for $3.00 discounts. Is there some sort of science going on here? Presumably, someone who converts all three coupons of descending value would be more brand-loyal than someone who converts the $3.00 ones. But who knows? In general, the appearance of science in direct marketing is seldom buttressed by reality.

The questionnaires are short, and smoking-oriented. None of the general lifestyle questions of yore, possibly on the advice of lawyers. The second package, interestingly, asks, "Do you smoke cigars?" a question seemingly at odds with the delicate, hyper-feminine style of the promotion.

Cigarettes Are Not Addictive!

Two mailing pieces from Carlton are just as well-crafted and diabolical, although not as warm and fuzzy as the Capri executions (if you'll forgive the term).

In each piece, an attractive businesswoman gazes confidently at the reader, declaring "The decision to smoke is mine" and "It's my decision to smoke. . . ." Inside, a box of Carltons pops up as you open the mailer, and the models, in half-body shots, declare ". . . and Carlton is my choice." Each piece offers five $2.00 coupons, with the final coupon beating a $1.00 discount. If there's any science here, the final redemption of the $1.00 coupon no doubt indicates someone who has decidedly switched to Carlton.

That's it, a most minimal approach in comparison with Capri.

Let's deconstruct this a bit.

"The decision to smoke is mine," supported by the clear-eyed, confident gaze of the model, is a sort of ghostly echo of the old Virginia Slims campaign, which tried its darndest to co-opt the women's liberation movement. And, indeed, there's always been an odd and uneasy relationship between feminism and smoking: George Sands' cigars in the mid-1800s, the factory girls smoking in "Carmen." In the U.S., smoking for females was popularized in the 1920s by Edward Bernays, the self-proclaimed father of public relations, who paid attractive women to march down 5th Avenue, boldly puffing on cigarettes. Just now, the American tobacco manufacturers, using some of Bernays' techniques, have made smoking fashionable among young Japanese women. They're less subtle in other parts of Asia: In 1996, I watched in horror as pretty young girls handed out sample packs of Marlboros to kids of both sexes in Kuala Lumpur's Central Market. . . .

> *"Brown & Williamson falls back on the oldest cigarette marketing trick in the book in a campaign for Capri: Cigarettes are good for you."*

Choice or Addiction?

"The decision to smoke is mine" is a nicely economical phrase, doing double duty as a sort of dated feminist manifesto and as a bald-faced denial of reality.

The trouble with cigarette smoking is you can turn it on, but you can't turn it off. The decision to start smoking may be mine, but continuing to smoke has nothing to do with choice, and everything to do with nicotine addiction, as the manufacturers themselves have finally kind of, sort of, admitted.

Referring to cigarette smoking as a "choice" is both a most primitive and a most powerful sort of obfuscation, because it blends denial with the Big Lie. Denial is the primordial defense mechanism, practiced by infants, politicians and other undeveloped beings. And nothing is more powerful than the Big Lie. . . .

Not to get too heavy about all this, but [this] reminds me of the eternal philosophical issue, can bad people create good art? They can, of course, and they sometimes do. Direct mail is way removed from art, but one is impressed by the superior craft of these Brown & Williamson mailing pieces. . . .

I wonder endlessly, though, about the people who produce these things. . . . Are they sociopathic? Are they clueless? Do they buy into the kitchen rationalizations of big tobacco? ("It's a legal product, it's a lifestyle choice.") Or are they merely numbed denizens of post-industrial capitalism, marching blindly in the dark?

Tobacco Ads Target Children

by Richard W. Pollay

About the author: *Richard W. Pollay teaches advertising and marketing management at the University of British Columbia.*

The standard response of the industry to concerns about children and cigarette advertising has been to insist that [as stated by R.J. Reynolds] "kids just don't pay attention to cigarette ads . . . (Our advertising) purpose is to get smokers of competitive products to switch . . . virtually the only way a cigarette brand can meaningfully increase its business," a thesis uncritically echoed by some others. The belief and assertion is that cigarette advertising is of little consequence, at least with respect to the young. This assertion, so counter to common sense, is argued on theoretical grounds. Because cigarettes seem to be a so-called "mature" industry, i.e., one which has completed its dynamic growth and reached a stasis, it is claimed that its advertising and promotional activity can and does affect only brand-switching behavior among established adult smokers. By neither intent nor effect, tobacco industry magnates would have us believe, does cigarette advertising influence young people, reassure and retain existing smokers who might otherwise quit, or induce current smokers to smoke more—several of the ways in which advertising might conceivably influence primary demand. . . .

Recruiting New Clients

The cigarette market may seem, to the naive, to be stable and, therefore, to be a so-called "mature market" because total sales seem nearly constant. This appearance, however, hides the dynamics of substantial rates of quitting attempts, quitting successes, and dying—and the countervailing rates of recruitment of hundreds of thousands of new smokers. Maintaining constancy of market size involves recruiting over a million new smokers a year, and almost all smokers are recruited as minors, not as consenting adults.

Brand-switching alone cannot easily justify the enormous advertising and promotional expenditures, over $6 billion a year in 1993, larger than Hollywood's gross income from the United States and Canada combined. Brand switchers are an unattractive market segment, as they are typically older, health-concerned, or symptomatic smokers, thus relatively frail in constitution, in addition to being fickle by definition. They are also few in number. . . . Less than 10 percent of smokers will switch in any given year . . . [and] the total profit from all "company switching" was $362 million in 1996, small compared to the costs of the battle of these brands. Accounting for sales in future years, the net present value of a new smoker to the cigarette companies has been estimated as US $1,085.

If cigarette advertising had no effect on smoking recruitment, as the industry contends, a ban on advertising expenditures of this magnitude should and would be welcomed by savvy oligopolists like the tobacco industry. Indeed, a ban would benefit the larger firms the most, by saving them the enormous promotional expense and helping to freeze their large market shares. Thus, if advertising had no effect on primary demand, profit-maximizing firms and industries would curtail advertising competition, just as they would refrain from cut-throat price competition, and the largest firms would be expected to act as leaders in this self-restraint. Failing a tacit collusion to this end, the industry would eagerly seize the opportunity provided by regulatory proposals to ban advertising, with the larger firms the most motivated to do so. The fact that cigarette companies, led by the largest, are lobbying so hard against advertising bans or controls of any kind is illogical—unless the advertising and promotion has the effect of enticing new smokers. As Ronald M. Davis stated: "The reason for the industry's failure to support a federal ban on tobacco advertising must be that . . . the companies must indeed perceive an industry-wide benefit to advertising and promotion." Failing that, they could save themselves all the spending on advertising that only attacked or defended market shares. . . .

Biased Perceptions and Attractive Imagery

Cigarette advertising is so pervasive and ubiquitous that cigarettes are a cultural commonplace, taken for granted by the public, and treated as less risky than appropriate. We are all aware of the reverse of this. When we feel suspicion of the unfamiliar. This positive effect is called "friendly familiarity" by advertising professionals. . . .

The young do, in fact, overestimate the prevalence of cigarette smoking among both peers and adults, and the

> *"Almost all smokers are recruited as minors, not as consenting adults."*

degree of this overestimation is among the strongest predictors of smoking initiation. They also underestimate the negative attitudes of peers and the risks to which they personally are exposed should they smoke. Youths are also inclined to manifest [what Leilani Greening and Stephen Dollinger call] an "invulnerability syndrome." Youths tend to both "exaggerate the social benefit (by overestimating the prevalence and popularity of smoking among peers and adults) and to underestimate the risks (by underestimating the prevalence of negative attitudes toward smoking held by their peers)" [according to Richard Bonnie and B. Lynch]. Another literature review concludes that "cigarette advertising appears to influence young people's perceptions of the pervasiveness, image, and function of smoking. Since misperceptions in these areas constitute psychosocial risk factors for the initiation of smoking, cigarette advertising appears to increase young people's risk of smoking" [according to the U.S. Department of Health and Human Services]. These facts seriously undermine the notion that the uptake of smoking is an informed choice or decision. Irrespective of this naivete, it is a misbehavior of minors, not consenting adults.

Cigarette ads often feature veritable pictures of health, depicting bold and lively behavior typically in pure and pristine outdoor environments. The images of cigarette ads portray themes known to appeal to young people, such as independence, adventure seeking, social approval, and sophistication. The theme of independence, in particular, so well captured by the Marlboro Man, strikes a responsive chord with the dominant psychological need of adolescents for autonomy and freedom from authority. Adolescent girls feel the same needs for autonomy as do boys, accounting for the otherwise surprising popularity of the Marlboro brand among girls. Motivation research confirms the insights of previous advertisers

> *"Cigarette advertising is so pervasive and ubiquitous that cigarettes are a cultural commonplace."*

and public relations professionals in seeing smoking as an expression of freedom and worldliness for women. It seems no coincidence that marketers of female brands "try to tap the emerging independence and self-fulfilment of women, to make smoking a badge to express that" [as stated by Waldman].

In addition, some of the models in cigarette advertisements appear particularly youthful. This isn't all that common, however, as cigarette firms know that teens desire symbols of adulthood, not symbols of youth (e.g., hard rock vs. "bubble gum" music). Imagery-based ads are potentially insidious, in contrast to verbal assertions which require cognitive processing. Imagery is taken in at a glance, experienced more than thought about, tending to "bypass logical analysis." Because of this, imagery advertising is deemed "transformational" rather than informational [as stated by S. Cohen]. The old adage says "seeing is believing," and cigarette ads use carefully tuned images to create positive experiences, while being careful to avoid precipitating cognitive counter-argumentation.

A Strategic Interest in Youth

The industry has demonstrated an interest in the youth market in its planning documents, market research activities, and media plans for many decades. Ads have been placed on billboards near schools and malls, and in after-school radio spots with effective reach into youth markets. The TV advertising schedules bought in the 1960s reflected a preference for those times with the higher pro-portions of delivered teenagers, not adults. R.J. Reynolds' 1973 "Re-search Planning Document on Some Thoughts about New Brands for the Youth Market" described programs for appealing to "learning smokers" [according to Jerome Schwartz]. Philip Morris found that almost half of the nonsmoking girls "share many

> *"The images of cigarette ads portray themes known to appeal to young people, such as independence, adventure seeking, social approval, and sophistication."*

of the same values as the smokers—and are highly exposed to the total smoking environment. We call them the 'Vulnerables' for, on the surface, they appear to be ready candidates for the next wave of new smokers" [as stated by Dr. Al Udow in 1976].

Copy concepts for many brands focus on independence, with the adolescent need for autonomy and self-reliance known by the industry to be a dominant one. The success of starter brands, according to trial evidence, is the result of carefully planned and executed strategies, guided throughout by extensive re-search. Corporate research documents discuss the behavior, knowledge, and at-titudes of eleven-, twelve-, and thirteen-year-olds, and media plans specify tar-gets beginning at age fifteen, with willingness to pay as much for ad exposures to fifteen-year-old nonsmokers as to smokers. R.J. Reynolds' Canadian affiliate, for example, commissioned customization of "Youth Target Study '87" and got extensive data on subjects as young as fifteen.

The need to have a strategic interest in youth has long been recognized by the industry, and used to be freely admitted to. For example, just before the Surgeon General's Report of 1964, an advertising trade magazine, *Sponsor*, noted pro-health education with concern and asked: "If, however, impression-able youngsters are now approached mostly by the anti-smoking fraternity, how will cigarette sales fare 10 years hence?" Note, too, that this also demon-strates the long time spans appropriate in understanding cigarette advertising's effects, which are generational rather than instantaneous, inculcative rather than impulse-generating.

Identity Formation and Advertising Attentiveness

[According to S. Chapman and B. Fitzgerald,] "Cigarette advertising's cul-tural function is much more than the selling of cigarettes. Its collective images represent a corpus of deeply rooted cultural mythologies that are not simply pieces of advertising creativity, but icons that pose solutions to real, experienced problems of identity." The National Association of Broadcasters knew this when trying to help the industry self-regulate TV ads. [In 1966, Al Bell stated,] "The adult world depicted in cigarette advertising very often is a world to which the adolescent aspires. . . . To the young, smoking indeed may seem to be an important step towards, and a help in growth from adolescence to maturity."

Youths are alert to popular culture for cues and clues as to what's hot and what's not. They attend to advertising for symbols of adulthood, but pay only scant attention to warnings. [According to M. Nichter and E. Cartwright,] "Teens are also more susceptible to the images of romance, success, sophistication, popularity, and adventure which advertising suggests they could achieve through the consumption of cigarettes." Even brief cigarette ad exposures in lab settings can result in more favorable thoughts about smokers, enhance attitudes, increase awareness and change brand preferences of the young.

This is consistent with consumer behavior knowledge as reflected in textbooks and journals. "Teenagers have become increasingly aware of new products and brands. They are natural 'triers'." [state David Loudon and Alberta Della Bitta]. They have "a lot of uncertainty about the self. and the need to belong and to find one's unique identity . . . (so) teens actively search for cues from their peers and from advertising for the right way to look and behave . . . (becoming) interested in many different products" that can express their needs for "experimentation, belonging, independence, responsibility, and approval from others," [as stated by L.J. Solomon]. By high school, possessions and [what B.G. Stacy calls] "badge products" like cigarettes are used as instruments for defining and controlling relations between people.

As a 1974 RJR [R.J. Reynolds] memo states: "To some extent young smokers 'wear' their cigarette, and it becomes an important part of the 'I' they wish to be, along with their clothing and the way they style their hair," [according to Jerome Schwartz]. One starter brand in Canada, according to the R.J. Reynolds affiliate who marketed it, was popular with "very young starter smokers . . . because it provides them with an instant badge of masculinity, appeals to their rebellious nature and establishes their position amongst their peers," [as stated by R.W. Pollay and A. Lavack]. Adults, in contrast, are not caught up in the processes of identity experimentation and formation. They are not as searching of their environment for consumption items symbolic of aspirational identities. . . .

Youths Are Strategically More Attractive than Adults

The trade of these older customers offers firms very little future and net present value, compared with the value inherent in attracting young starters, the bulk of whom will be brand-loyal. [Loudon and Della Bitta state,] "This is a time when brand loyalties may be formed that could last well into adulthood." The young are a "perpetually new market . . . thus a marketer must not neglect young consumers who come 'on stream' if the company's brand is to have continued success in the older-age market." Teens are a strategically important target audience, because brand loyalty is often developed during this time and this creates a "barrier-to-entry for other brands not chosen during these pivotal years."

The death and quitting rates among aging smokers means that sales would drop rapidly were it not for a continuing influx of new starters. This strategic situation has been obvious to the industry for some time. R.J. Reynolds' research and development officers wrote in 1973: [According to Schwartz], "Realistically, if our Company is to survive and prosper, over the long term, we must get our share of the youth market." Contemporary corporate documents echo this idea, stating that "young smokers represent the major opportunity group for the cigarette industry," and "if the last ten years have taught us anything, it is that the industry is dominated by the companies who respond most effectively to the needs of younger smokers," [as stated by Pollay and Lavack].

The latest research uses state-of-the-art techniques to analyze market share as a function of relative advertising, also known as share of voice. This measures the impact of cigarette brand advertising on realized market shares, allowing for both current and historical effects of advertising for nine major brands over twenty years. The results, which are robust under many alternative assumptions, show that brand choices among teenagers are significantly related to relative cigarette advertising. Moreover, the relationship between brand choices and brand advertising is significantly stronger among teenagers than among adults by a factor of about three. The greater advertising sensitivity among teenagers is in part due to scale (i.e., high fractions of teens concentrated on highly advertised brands), and in part due to dynamics (i.e., teen purchase patterns being more responsive to changes in advertising intensity). Further, the impact of advertising on brand choices among youth apparently cannot be dismissed as an inappropriate attribution (i.e., teenagers actually imitating adult brand choices rather than responding to advertising). Even when this aspect is factored into the analysis, the result remains consistent.

Greater advertising sensitivity among youth is consistent with earlier observations that brand choices of youth are highly concentrated on the most heavily advertised brands. California's Operation Storefront also found that "heavy advertising in stores exactly matches the brand preferences of children who smoke . . . but the ad prevalence does not match adult smoker preferences," [according to P. Hilts]. [K. Rombouts and G. Fauconnier state,] "Young people know advertising better, appreciate brand-stretching advertising more," and their ideal self-image matches the images offered by cigarette brands. A 1995 study reported data indicating that smoking rates among young women increased sharply in the late 1960s, coincidental with the launch of Virginia Slims and other nominally "female" brands. . . .

Given the many various analyses and diversity of evidence, it seems an inescapable conclusion that cigarette advertising plays a meaningful role in influencing the perceptions, attitudes, and smoking behavior of youth. It also seems appropriate for scholars to react to assertions that there are no such effects on youth with disbelief, and to suspect industry sponsorship as a likely basis for such assertions.

Smoking in Movies Increases Cigarette Consumption

by Stanton Glantz

About the author: *Stanton Glantz is a professor of medicine and cardiology at the University of California, San Francisco.*

Fighting secondhand smoke for nearly 25 years, I've learned the enemy isn't the poor smoker. It's the tobacco industry. Big Tobacco knows its future riches depend, more than anything else, on social acceptance. Without it, ashtrays will go the way of the spittoon. But acceptance must be constantly manufactured. And Hollywood has always been in on the act.

Soon after I started working for clean indoor air, I realized the reason that clean indoor air was such a crucial issue to the tobacco industry was that smoking restrictions of any kind undermined the social acceptability of smoking and made it harder for the tobacco industry to recruit new smokers and keep current smokers addicted. In contrast to the health groups, who saw smoking as a medical issue, the tobacco industry has always seen smoking as a cultural issue.

And there is no better way to control pop culture worldwide than through movies. Tobacco mass marketing and Hollywood pop culture grew up together, businesslike twins joined at the hip. For 80 years the tobacco industry has addicted hundreds of millions of men and women with the help of Hollywood movies—and, later, TV—that portrayed smoking as glamorous, sexy, adult. Stars once explicitly endorsed tobacco brands in magazine ads and TV commercials. Now they implicitly endorse brands by using them in the movies. There's actually been an upswing in movie smoking over the last few years. Is it corruption? Or stupidity?

It's the rich, powerful and glamorous who smoke in the movies, when in reality it's the depressed, poor and less educated who smoke. It doesn't matter if the good guys or the bad guys smoke. Large studies have shown that the more smoking in the movies kids see, the more likely they are to start smoking. . . .

Evading the Television Ban

The secret history [of Hollywood and Big Tobacco], uncovered in tons of corporate files produced by recent lawsuits, shows the two industries colluded to get around the 1970 TV ban on tobacco advertising. L.A.'s biggest public relations firms brokered endorsements with some of the film industry's biggest names. Publicity was bought for as little as free cartons. This hasn't stopped. *Vanity Fair*'s Oscar party in 2001 featured bowls of free cigarettes, whose generous donors hoped paparazzi would snap the smoking stars. . . .

The handshake deal was to keep big stars publicly smoking, place tobacco brands on the scene and include tobacco advertising in the frame. Just as important, the tobacco industry pushed negative images out. On-screen smoking was supposed to project fantasies of sexuality and power, good or bad, always dramatic—never the ugly, banal realities of addiction, disease and death.

As you might expect, the seduction was mutual. Here's how one producer shrewdly, accurately pitched RJ Reynolds: "Film is better than any commercial that has been run on television or in any magazine because the audience is totally unaware of any sponsor involvement."

By the late 1980s, things got so giddy that one star agreed to take $500,000 from Brown & Williamson Tobacco to show its brands in his next five movies. Meanwhile, rival Philip Morris agreed to pay $350,000 to have James Bond smoke Larks. Even Superman was implicated—Lois Lane chain-smoked Marlboros and Superman II saved the world by bursting from a giant Marlboro logo.

Shaken by congressional hearings on such shenanigans in 1989, Big Tobacco promised to stop paying for smoking in the movies. They promised again in 1998 when they settled tobacco litigation brought by the states.

Smoking in Movies Has Increased

But the plot has only thickened since then. There is actually more smoking in the movies now than 10 years ago, before the tobacco industry's voluntary ban on smoking in the movies. And the brands most heavily advertised in other media are the ones most likely to show up on the big screen. Hollywood covets the 18-to-24-year-old demographic, and so does Big Tobacco. Coincidence? Marlboro scores the most screen appearances in Hollywood movies; it also owns the market of young, new smokers.

U.S. teens aren't the only victims. Hollywood movies offer a major marketing vehicle for Big Tobacco overseas. Outside the American media spotlight, celebrities such as Antonio Banderas and Charlie Sheen

> *"Big Tobacco knows its future riches depend, more than anything else, on social acceptance."*

have shilled for Parliament (Philip Morris, yet again) in TV spots and print ads from Japan to Argentina. How can we possibly believe that Hollywood has sworn off Big Tobacco?

Tobacco companies are longtime liars and deniers, so we can hardly turn to them for candor. As late as 1994, their executives swore under oath that nicotine wasn't addictive. They certainly didn't come fully clean about their Hollywood connections in 1989. But what about the Hollywood community? Why is it serving a racket that's buried many of its most gifted members and continues to kill 3 million people each year?

> *"Film is better than any commercial that has been run on television or in any magazine because the audience is totally unaware of any sponsor involvement."*

Perhaps we should pity A-list stars who confuse their own addictions with valid artistic choices—and insist on smoking while cameras roll. Maybe we should cock a cliched eyebrow at directors and writers who lazily rely on what Stella Adler called "cigarette acting" to build character. Or maybe we should ask if Hollywood studios—many of them now part of huge media conglomerates—are quietly stroking the tobacco industry for advertising heavily in magazines belonging to the same corporate litter. Payola, after all, is effective only if it can't be seen.

Raising Consciousness

Because of concern over the growing pro-tobacco influence of movies, I have spent the last 10 years quietly attending meetings and conferences with people from the entertainment industry trying to "raise consciousness" about this problem. As a professor, I also value creativity and intellectual freedom and hoped to make progress through quiet discussion. While I met many good people, the power structure in the movie industry simply repeated the same sort of hackneyed arguments about the 1st Amendment that we hear so often from their friends in the tobacco industry. This isn't about the 1st Amendment or freedom of expression, and the solution isn't censorship, a cure as bad as the disease.

We know people were crassly paid off in the past. We know there's more smoking in movies now than before. We also know that smoking doesn't sell movie tickets. It sells cigarettes to kids who watch PG-13- and R-rated movies and videos. Knowing all that—and knowing Big Tobacco so well—I propose four modest but effective fixes:

- Certify in the end credits that nobody on the production received anything of value—cash, loans, smokes, publicity, nada—in exchange for using or displaying tobacco.
- Require genuinely strong anti-tobacco advertisements—not produced by the tobacco industry or its fronts—to run before films with any tobacco presence. This will help immunize audiences without intruding on the film's content.
- Stop identifying brands. For leads like Nicolas Cage, Angelina Jolie, Brad Pitt or Julia Roberts to smoke a Marlboro or any other brand on screen is worth far, far more to Big Tobacco than a traditional advertisement.

• Rate any film with smoking an R. Kids who start smoking say they expect to quit within five years. They don't. One-third will eventually die from to-bacco—far more than from gun violence, let alone foul language in a film.

None of these four measures requires government action. None will choke creativity or restrict content. Each will make American movies much less complicit in the global tobacco epidemic.

Now what's the excuse?

Advertising by Tobacco Companies Does Not Influence People to Smoke

by Jacob Sullum

About the author: *Jacob Sullum is a senior editor for* Reason *magazine, a monthly journal of libertarian opinion.*

On January 1, 1971, the Marlboro Man rode across the television screen one last time. At midnight a congressional ban on broadcast advertising of cigarettes went into effect, and the smoking cowboy was banished to the frozen land of billboards and print ads. With the deadline looming, bleary-eyed, hungover viewers across the country woke to a final burst of cigarette celebration. "Philip Morris went on a $1.25-million ad binge New Year's Day on the Dick Cavett, Johnny Carson and Merv Griffin shows," *The New York Times* reported. "There was a surfeit of cigarette ads during the screening of the bowl games." And then they were gone. American TV viewers would no longer be confronted by happy smokers frolicking on the beach or by hapless smokers losing the tips of their extra-long cigarettes between cymbals and elevator doors. They would no longer have to choose between good grammar and good taste.

This was widely considered an important victory for consumers. *The Times* wondered whether the ad ban was "a signal that the voice of the consumer, battling back, can now really make itself heard in Washington." A *New Yorker* article tracing the chain of events that led to the ban concluded, "To an increasing degree, citizens of the consumer state seem to be perceiving their ability to turn upon their manipulators, to place widespread abuses of commercial privilege under the prohibition of laws that genuinely do protect the public, and, in effect, to give back to the people a sense of controlling their own lives."

As these comments suggest, supporters of the ban viewed advertising not as a form of communication but as a mysterious force that seduces people into acting against their interests. This was a common view then and now, popularized by social critics such as Vance Packard and John Kenneth Galbraith. In *The Affluent Society* (1958), Galbraith argued that manufacturers produce goods and then apply "ruthless psychological pressures" through advertising to create demand for them. In *The Hidden Persuaders* (1957), Packard described advertising as an increasingly precise method of manipulation that can circumvent the conscious mind, influencing consumers without their awareness. He reinforced his portrait of Madison Avenue guile with the pseudoscientific concept of subliminal messages: seen but not seen, invisibly shaping attitudes and actions. The impact of such ideas can be seen in the controversy over tobacco advertising. The federal court that upheld the ban on broadcast ads for cigarettes quoted approvingly from another ruling that referred to "the subliminal impact of this pervasive propaganda.". . .

Today's critics of capitalism continue to elaborate on the theme that Vance Packard and John Kenneth Galbraith got so much mileage out of in the '50s and '60s. Alan Thein Durning of the anti-growth Worldwatch Institute describes the "salient characteristics" of advertising this way: "It preys on the weaknesses of its host. It creates an insatiable hunger. And it leads to debilitating over-consumption. In the biological realm, things of that nature are called parasites." When combined with appeals to protect children, this perception of advertising as insidious and overpowering tends to squelch any lingering concerns about free speech.

Busting Joe Camel's Hump

In 1988 R.J. Reynolds gave the anti-smoking movement an emblem for the corrupting influence of tobacco advertising. Introduced with the slogan "smooth character," Joe Camel was a cartoon version of the dromedary (known as Old Joe) that has appeared on packages of Camel cigarettes since 1913. Print ads and billboards depicted Joe Camel shooting pool in a tuxedo, hanging out at a nightclub, playing in a blues band, sitting on a motorcycle in a leather jacket and shades. He was portrayed as cool, hip, and popular—in short, he was like a lot of other models in a lot of other cigarette ads, except he was a cartoon animal instead of a flesh-and-blood human being. Even in that respect he was hardly revolutionary. More than a century before the debut of Joe Camel, historian Jordan Goodman notes, the manufacturer of Bull Durham smoking tobacco ran newspaper ads throughout

> *"[The] perception of advertising as insidious and overpowering tends to squelch any lingering concerns about free speech."*

the country depicting the Durham Bull "in anthropomorphic situations, alternating between scenes in which the bull was jovial and boisterous and those where he was serious and determined."

But Joe Camel, it is safe to say, generated more outrage than any other cartoon character in history. Critics of the ad campaign said the use of a cartoon was clearly designed to appeal to children. *Washington Post* columnist Courtland Milloy said "packaging a cartoon camel as a 'smooth character' is as dangerous as putting rat poison in a candy wrapper." In response to such criticism, R.J. Reynolds noted that Snoopy sold life insurance and the Pink Panther pitched fiberglass insulation, yet no one assumed those ads were aimed at kids.

The controversy intensified in 1991, when *The Journal of the American Medical Association* published three articles purporting to show that Joe Camel was indeed a menace to the youth of America. The heavily promoted studies generated an enormous amount of press coverage, under headlines such as "Camels for Kids" (*Time*), "I'd Toddle a Mile for a Camel" (*Newsweek*), "Joe Camel Is Also Pied Piper, Research Finds" (*The Wall Street Journal*), and "Study: Camel Cartoon Sends Kids Smoke Signals" (*Boston Herald*). Dozens of editorialists and columnists condemned Joe Camel, and many said he should be banned from advertising. . . .

The Burden of Proof

[None of the three] studies provided any evidence about the impact of advertising on a teenager's propensity to smoke, which is the crux of the issue. When critics complain that advertising encourages people to smoke, the tobacco companies reply that it encourages smokers to buy particular brands. Strictly speaking, these claims are not mutually exclusive. In principle, advertising can promote an industry's overall sales as well as drum up business for a specific company.

> *"[No] studies provided any evidence about the impact of advertising on a teenager's propensity to smoke."*

An ad for a Compaq portable computer might encourage people to buy a Compaq (the company certainly hopes so), or it might get them thinking about laptops generally. But the tobacco companies argue that the U.S. market for cigarettes is mature, meaning that the product is universally familiar, like toothpaste or deodorant, and attempts to boost overall consumption are no longer cost-effective. Indeed, with smoking rates declining, the tobacco companies are fighting for pieces of a shrinking pie. Tobacco's opponents say this trend makes cigarette manufacturers all the more desperate to maintain their profits; they need advertising like the Joe Camel campaign to attract replacements for smokers who quit or die.

Advocates of an advertising ban contend that brand competition does not adequately explain the industry's spending on advertising and promotion, which totals about $5 billion a year. In 1995, the most recent year for which the Federal Trade Commission (FTC) has reported figures, coupons, customer premiums (lighters, key chains, clothing, etc.), and allowances to distributors accounted for about 80 percent of this money. Cigarette companies spent about $900 million on newspaper, magazine, outdoor, transit, direct-mail, and point-of-sale advertising.

According to a widely cited article published in the Winter 1987 *Journal of Public Health Policy*, "A simple calculation shows that brand-switching, alone, could never justify the enormous advertising and promotional expenditures of the tobacco companies." Anti-smoking activist Joe B. Tye and his co-authors started with an estimate, based on marketing research, that about 10 percent of smokers switch brands each year. Then they calculated that the industry's spending on advertising and promotion in 1983 amounted to nearly as much per switcher as a typical smoker would have spent on cigarettes that year. They also noted that, since each cigarette maker produces various brands, smokers who switch are not necessarily taking their business to another company.

> *"Building brand loyalty among teenagers is still not the same thing as making them into smokers."*

"Thus," the authors concluded, "advertising and promotion can be considered economically rational only if they perform a defensive function—retaining company brand loyalty that would otherwise be lost to competitors who promote their products—or if they attract new entrants to the smoking marketplace, or discourage smokers from quitting." If defending market share were the only aim, Tye et al. added, the tobacco companies should support a ban on advertising and promotion, which would eliminate the threat from competitors. On the other hand, "If advertising and promotion increase cigarette consumption, then less than two million new or retained smokers—5.5 percent of smokers who start each year or try to quit (most failing)—alone would justify the annual promotional expenditure."

Accounting for Variables

There are several flaws in this argument. To begin with, the estimate for the number of brand switchers does not include people who usually smoke, say, Benson & Hedges but occasionally smoke Camels. Based on its own marketing surveys, R.J. Reynolds reports that about 70 percent of smokers have a second-choice brand that they smoke now and then. About 25 percent regularly buy more than one brand each month. Even smokers who don't have a second favorite sometimes try other brands because of coupons, premiums, and promotional offers.

Another problem is that, in estimating the value of brand switchers, Tye et al. did not take into account the continuing revenue from a new customer; they considered only the money he spends on cigarettes in one year. By contrast, when they estimated the gain from getting someone to start smoking or keeping a smoker who otherwise would have quit, they used the net present value of the additional profit over a 20-year period, which they calculated as

$1,085, more than three times a year's revenue.

Most important, Tye et al. did not acknowledge that tobacco companies could be competing for new smokers without actually creating them. Although the companies deny that they target minors in any way, building brand loyalty among teenagers is still not the same thing as making them into smokers. . . .

In any case, it is not clearly foolish for the tobacco companies to spend so much money on advertising and promotion, even without the hope of market expansion. More evidence is necessary to support the claim that tobacco advertising increases consumption. Broadly speaking, there are three ways of investigating this issue. You can look at the historical relationship between changes in advertising and changes in smoking. You can compare smoking trends in places with different levels of advertising. And you can ask people questions in the hope that their answers will suggest how advertising influences attitudes and behavior. None of these approaches has yielded consistent or definitive results. Each has limitations that leave plenty of room for interpretation. The state of the research was aptly, if unintentionally, summed up by the subtitle of a 1994 article in the *International Journal of Advertising* that made the case for a causal link: "The Evidence Is There for Those Who Wish to See It."

Does Life Imitate Ads?

Some analyses of historical data have found a small, statistically significant association between increases in advertising and increases in smoking; others have not. In a 1993 overview of the evidence, Michael Schudson, professor of communication and sociology at the University of California at San Diego, wrote, "In terms of a general relationship between cigarette advertising and cigarette smoking, the available econometric evidence is equivocal and the kind of materials available to produce the evidence leave much to be desired." This sort of research is open to challenge on technical grounds, such as the time period chosen and the methods for measuring advertising and consumption. There is also the possibility that advertising goes up in response to a rise in consumption, rather than the reverse. Industry critics often cite the increases in smoking by women that occurred in the 1920s and the late '60s to early '70s as evidence of advertising's power. "Yet in both cases," Schudson noted, "the advertising campaign followed rather than preceded the behavior it supposedly engendered." In other words, the tobacco companies changed their marketing in response to a trend that was already under way.

> *"Smokers themselves rarely cite advertising as an important influence on their behavior."*

International comparisons have also produced mixed results. There is no consistent relationship between restrictions on advertising and smoking rates among adults or minors. In some countries where advertising is severely restricted, such as Sweden, smoking rates are relatively low. In others, such as Norway, they are relatively high. Sometimes smoking drops after advertising is banned; sometimes it doesn't. It is hard to say what such findings mean. Countries where smoking is already declining may be more intolerant of the habit and therefore more likely to ban advertising. Alternatively, a rise in smoking might help build support for a ban. Furthermore, advertising bans are typically accompanied by other measures, such as tobacco tax increases and restrictions on smoking in public, that could be expected to reduce cigarette purchases. The one conclusion it seems safe to draw is that many factors other than advertising affect tobacco consumption.

The best way to resolve the issue of advertising's impact on smoking would be a controlled experiment: Take two groups of randomly selected babies; expose one to cigarette advertising but otherwise treat them identically. After 18 years or so, compare smoking rates. Since such a study would be impractical, social scientists have had to make do with less tidy methods, generally involving interviews, questionnaires, or survey data. This kind of research indicates that the most important factors influencing whether a teenager will smoke are the behavior of his peers, his perceptions of the risks and benefits of smoking, and the presence of smokers in his home. Exposure to advertising does not independently predict the decision to smoke, and smokers themselves rarely cite advertising as an important influence on their behavior.

> *"The evidence that advertising plays an important role in getting people to smoke is not very convincing."*

Advertising Affects Brand Choice

Critics of the industry have been quick to seize upon studies indicating that teenage smokers disproportionately prefer the most advertised cigarette brands. But such research suggests only that advertising has an impact on brand preferences, which the tobacco companies have conceded all along. Several studies have found that teenagers who smoke (or who say they might) are more apt to recall cigarette advertising and to view it favorably. Such findings do not necessarily mean that advertising makes adolescents more likely to smoke. It is just as plausible to suppose that teenagers pay more attention to cigarette ads after they start smoking, or that teenagers who are inclined to smoke for other reasons are also more likely to have a positive view of cigarette ads.

In reporting on research in this area, the mainstream press tends to ignore such alternative interpretations. Consider the coverage of a 1995 study published in the *Journal of the National Cancer Institute*. The study, co-authored by John Pierce, found that teenagers who scored high on a "receptivity" index—which included "recognition of advertising messages, having a favorite advertisement, naming a brand [they] might buy, owning a tobacco-related promotional item, and willingness to use a tobacco-related promotional item"—were more likely to say they could not rule out smoking in the near future. Such "receptivity" was more strongly associated with an inclination to smoke than was smoking among parents and peers.

According to *The New York Times*, these results meant that "[t]obacco advertising is a stronger factor than peer pressure in encouraging children under 18 to smoke." Similarly, *The Boston Globe* reported that the study showed "cigarette advertising has more influence on whether adolescents later start smoking than does having friends or family members who smoke." The Associated Press went even further: "Of all the influences that can draw children into a lifelong habit of smoking, cigarette advertising is the most persuasive." In reality, the study showed only that teenagers who like smoking-related messages and merchandise are more receptive to the idea of smoking—not exactly a startling finding.

A study reported in December 1997 in *Archives of Pediatric and Adolescent Medicine* received similar treatment. The researchers surveyed about 1,200 students in grades six through 12 and found that kids who owned cigarette promotional items such as jackets and backpacks were four times as likely to smoke as those who did not. "Tobacco Gear a Big Draw for Kids," announced the headline in *The Boston Globe*. The story began, "If tobacco manufacturers hope to promote smoking by producing clothing or accessories emblazoned with cigarette logos, research by Dartmouth Medical School suggests that the tactic works well." Under the headline, "Study: Logos Foster Smoking," *Newsday* reported that "children who own cigarette promotional items . . . are far more likely to smoke."

Yet as the researchers themselves conceded, "The finding of an association between CPI [cigarette promotional item] ownership and being a smoker could easily be an expression of an adolescent who acquired these items after having made the decision to become a smoker." Later in the article, they wrote, "Our study and others published to date are subject to the usual limitations inherent in cross-sectional studies, in that we are unable to infer a direction between the exposure (ownership of a CPI) and smoking behavior, limiting our ability to invoke a causal relationship between CPI ownership and smoking." Translation: We would like to say that promotional items make kids smoke, but our study doesn't show that. This shortcoming did not stop the authors from concluding that "all CPI distribution should end immediately."

Marginal Effects

Overall, the evidence that advertising plays an important role in getting people to smoke is not very convincing. In 1991 the economist Thomas Schelling, former director of Harvard's Institute for the Study of Smoking Behavior and Policy, said: "I've never seen a genuine study of the subject. Most of the discussion that I hear—even the serious discussion—is about as profound as saying, 'If I were a teenage black girl, that ad would make me smoke.' I just find it altogether unpersuasive. I've been very skeptical that advertising is important in either getting people to smoke or keeping people smoking. It's primarily brand competition." The 1989 surgeon general's report conceded that "[t]here is no scientifically rigorous study available to the public that provides a definitive answer to the basic question of whether advertising and promotion increase the level of tobacco consumption. Given the complexity of the issue, none is likely to be forthcoming in the foreseeable future." The 1994 surgeon general's report, which focused on underage smoking, also acknowledged the "lack of definitive literature."

> *"Despite the lack of evidence that advertising has a substantial impact on smoking rates, tobacco's opponents can argue that we should play it safe and ban the ads."*

It's possible, of course, that tobacco advertising has an effect that simply cannot be measured. The 1989 surgeon general's report concluded that, while "the extent of the influence of advertising and promotion on the level of consumption is unknown and possibly unknowable," the weight of the evidence "makes it more likely than not that advertising and promotional activities do stimulate cigarette consumption." The 1994 report, based on suggestive evidence, said "cigarette advertising appears to increase young people's risk of smoking." Similarly, Michael Schudson—who says "[a]dvertising typically attempts little and achieves still less"—argues that cigarette advertising "normally has only slight effect in persuading people to change their attitudes or behaviors." But he adds, "It is reasonable to believe that some teens become smokers or become smokers earlier or become smokers with less guilt or become heavier smokers because of advertising."

Serious critics of tobacco advertising do not subscribe to a simple stimulus-and-response theory in which kids exposed to Joe Camel automatically become smokers. They believe the effects of advertising are subtle and indirect. They argue that the very existence of cigarette ads suggests "it really couldn't be all that bad, or they wouldn't be allowed to advertise," as Elizabeth Whelan of the American Council on Science and Health puts it. They say advertising imagery reinforces the notion, communicated by peers and other role models, that smoking is cool. They say dependence on advertising revenue from tobacco companies discourages magazines from running articles about the health consequences of smoking. They do not claim such effects are sufficient, by themselves, to make people smoke. Rather, they argue that at the margin—say, for an ambivalent teenager whose friends smoke—the influence of advertising may be decisive.

Stated this way, the hypothesis that tobacco advertising increases consumption is impossible to falsify. "Fundamentally," writes Jean J. Boddewyn, a professor of marketing at Baruch College, "one cannot prove that advertising does not cause or influence smoking, because one cannot scientifically prove a negative." So despite the lack of evidence that advertising has a substantial impact on smoking rates, tobacco's opponents can argue that we should play it safe and ban the ads—just in case.

The problem with this line of reasoning is that banning tobacco advertising can be considered erring on the side of caution only if we attach little or no value to freedom of speech. If cigarette ads are a bad influence on kids, that is something for parents and other concerned adults to counter with information and exhortation. They might even consider a serious effort to enforce laws against cigarette sales to minors. But since we clearly are not helpless to resist the persuasive powers of Philip Morris et al.—all of us see the ads, but only some of us smoke—it is hard to square an advertising ban with a presumption against censorship. Surely a nation that proudly allows racist fulminations, communist propaganda, flag burning, nude dancing, pornography, and sacrilegious art can safely tolerate Marlboro caps and Joe Camel T-shirts.

Tobacco Ads Do Not Cause an Increase in Smoking

by Hugh High

About the author: *Hugh High is the director of the Program in Financial Analysis and Portfolio Management with the Faculty of Commerce at the University of Cape Town, South Africa.*

The conventional rationale of the right of government to restrict tobacco advertising is protection of the health of the citizenry and particularly of younger members of society who are alleged to be both particularly deserving of protection and particularly susceptible to the lure of commercial tobacco advertising.

We do not here enter into the question of the health effects of smoking tobacco products, but if a government believes that consumption of tobacco products impairs the health of consumers, we might understand it considering outlawing all consumption. Yet governments have not done so for a number of reasons. The general history of prohibition of alcohol, and other products, clearly demonstrates that it does not so much curb consumption as raise their prices and usually gives rise to various criminal acts related to sale of the prohibited product. The ill-fated history of American prohibition is well known to even the most ignorant parliamentarian.

Since in most Western countries, tobacco continues to be consumed by around a third of all adults who are also voters, outright prohibition would surely be met with the stiffest opposition. Furthermore, taxation of tobacco is an important source of government revenue. Consequently, instead of an outright ban on the sale and consumption of tobacco products, governments have responded with lesser political pressures, suggesting that governments do not find the health threat so dire as to justify prohibition.

Restrictions on Tobacco Advertising Are Recent

Interestingly, belief that tobacco advertising increases smoking is quite new. In 1975, Karl Warnberg of Sweden, addressing the Third World Conference on Smoking and Health, said:

No empirical research has been able to show that aggregate brand advertising leads to greater total tobacco consumption. Nor has anything been found to suggest that advertising entices non-smokers, young people in particular, into becoming smokers. It follows, therefore, that there can be no evidence that a ban on advertising would result in reduced tobacco consumption and fewer new smokers.

At this same conference Professor James L. Hamilton, a professor of Marketing at Wayne State University in Ohio, noted that cigarette advertising by tobacco companies was invariably employed as a 'competitive weapon' (against rival brands) and 'has not been used as a means for expanding the market'.

Similarly, in 1982, the Task Force on Smoking of the Province of Ontario, Canada, concluded that 'no persuasive empirical evidence exists' to support the argument that advertising is a significant determinant of smoking. This was followed in 1983 by the statement of Michael Pertschuk, former Chairman of the US Federal Trade Commission—who now assists the anti-smoking Advocacy Institute—that 'no one really pretends that advertising is a . . . major determinant of smoking in this country'. In 1985, Elizabeth Whelan of the American Council on Health doubted that an advertising ban would reduce cigarette consumption.

> *"'No persuasive empirical evidence exists' to support the argument that advertising is a significant determinant of smoking."*

Indeed, as recently as 1989 then US Surgeon General, C. Everett Koop, acknowledged that cigarette advertising and promotion had not been shown to increase tobacco consumption:

> There is no scientifically rigorous study available to the public that provides a definitive answer to the basic question of whether advertising and promotion increase the level of tobacco consumption.

Moreover, on smoking by young people, as early as 1969 data of the American Cancer Society presented to the US Congress demonstrated the power of example in shaping smoking behaviour: 'where parents or other frequently-seen adults smoke, youngsters are more likely to take up the habit. [Indeed] most influential of all seems to be friends.'

These observations were correct in suggesting no relationship between tobacco consumption and advertising either among adults or younger persons. It is difficult to understand why, aside from propaganda, those concerned about smoking should divert resources and attention to the effects of advertising.

The belief that advertising might lead to increased consumption or induce non-smokers to begin smoking is, like the invention of 'passive smoking', largely a product of the last decade or so.

Virtually all companies, including monopolies, advertise. Much of this advertising is not intended to increase the number of people who use the 'product category'. Rather, advertising is employed for a variety of reasons depending on whether the product is in a 'new product' category or a 'mature' one and on whether the product category is in competition with other categories.

With new product categories such as cellular telephones, videocassette recorders or personal computers, advertising aims to inform people about their general attributes and benefits, rather than to promote a particular *brand*. As consumer awareness of the product category expands, advertising faces a mature market. Examples of mature markets include petrol, toothpaste, soap, laundry detergent, telephones, and television sets. There is a large literature which demonstrates that in such mature markets advertising is not significantly related to aggregate product demand but aims to raise demand for the advertised brand. This fact was even acknowledged, as recently as 1994, by the US Institute of Medicine.

Nonetheless, it has been argued by some, including the American Food and Drug Administration (FDA), that cigarettes are not a mature market because the tobacco industry must continue to advertise so as to 'lure' young people into the market. This reflects a total failure to understand what is meant by a mature product.

The simple fact is that every mature market—whether automobiles, houses, television sets, cigarettes, washing machines, and so on—has first-time buyers who have never previously purchased the product. Manufacturers of cigarettes are no more dependent on new buyers than are other manufacturers of mature products. It is entirely rational for manufacturers of goods in mature markets to advertise in order to increase or maintain their existing market share. In the UK, total annual sales of cigarettes are over £12 billion so that gaining an additional 1 per cent share means gaining sales of well over £100 million.

Maintaining Brand Loyalty

The importance of maintaining market share is especially acute in the British tobacco industry which is faced by evidence that more than 1 in 3 smokers switch brands every year. Advertising, then, is a highly effective way to ensure that keen competition exists in the tobacco market-place which bans and restrictions on advertising can only stifle, thereby entrenching established firms.

In conclusion, it should be emphasised that were advertising of tobacco products to be banned, it would be more difficult for consumers to ac-

> *"Advertising . . . is a highly effective way to ensure that keen competition exists in the tobacco market-place."*

quire knowledge of new products, including cigarettes with lower tar and nicotine and so-called 'smokeless' cigarettes. It would therefore inhibit the development of such products, as well as making it more difficult for new entrants with 'specialised' products to enter the market. . . .

Children and Advertising

A rationale commonly advanced for regulating tobacco products is that smoking among the young is increased by advertising. While our concern here is not with trends in youth smoking, it is instructive to note that, as Peter van Doren has recently demonstrated, short-term trends in behaviour often mask longer term trends and give the appearance that youth smoking rates have changed. This illustrates the perils of focusing attention on short-run periods. When viewed over longer periods, 'the data demonstrates that the trend in youth smoking is rather benign' and that 'the alarmist view of smoking behaviour by minors is not consistent with the data over the last twenty years'.

Despite this important finding, it is frequently argued by advocates of advertising bans that even if advertising has little or no effect on consumption by adults, children are rather more impressionable and thus more likely to be affected by advertising. There are a number of problems with this argument. Advertising bans designed to protect children also deprive adults of the right to consume/enjoy commercial speech in the form of advertising which in turn precludes them from making informed decisions on tobacco products. Further, advertising restrictions make it difficult for new firms to enter the market, and thus deprive consumers of new and possibly more beneficial products, including lower tar/nicotine products. Moreover, a ban on advertising removes the incentive for established producers to develop such products as a response to competitive pressures, and thus discourages innovation in the market for tobacco products.

Leaving these and related arguments aside, there are a number of good reasons against advertising restrictions designed to protect children. An immense amount of evidence contradicts the surmise that people generally, and children particularly, begin consuming tobacco products as a result of advertising. Research demonstrates that the most important determinants of initiation into smoking are: (a) whether members of the family smoke, and (b) whether peers smoke.

Awareness Is Not Consumption

Advocates of restrictions are fond of pointing to studies showing that children are aware of various tobacco adverts, most prominently 'Joe Camel' and 'the Marlboro man'. Yet awareness hardly implies that the viewer will consume the product advertised, which would mean that advertisers have an automatic sales machine. The idea that consumers generally, and children in particular, are 'puppets of Madison Avenue' has no foundation in fact, despite the populist tirade of authors, such as John Kenneth Galbraith and Vance Packard. Serious academics in marketing and economics give such arguments little or no credence.

As we have seen, there are various reasons why some people are more aware of particular advertisements than others; the existence of 'selective perception' is well known in both psychology and marketing. As we shall see, there is ample evidence that children who are aware of advertising: (a) typically have family members who smoke, and (b) typically assert that, while aware of advertising, they have no intention of beginning to smoke. Perception is not consumption.

Without prejudging the health/medical arguments on smoking, tobacco companies are universally in the forefront of wishing to stop cigarettes being sold illegally to minors. It is at least likely that a ban would lead to a weakening of the effort to enforce the law against under-age smoking.

The Influence of Peers and Family

Family and friends are the major influences on smoking by the young. This has been widely acknowledged by governmental and university researchers around the globe. Indeed, it has been acknowledged by anti-smoking advocates, including evidence based on American Cancer Society data which concluded in 1969 from the available evidence that: 'Where parents or other frequently seen adults smoke, youngsters are more likely to take up the habit. . . . Most influential of all seem to be friends.'

This view was upheld in 1983 by the Director of the US National Institute of Child Health and Human Development in evidence given to the US House of Representatives:

> The most forceful determinants of smoking [by young people] are parents, peers, and older siblings. If one parent smokes, the child is twice as likely to smoke as one reared in a non-smoking household. If both parents smoke, the chances become four to one. If the child's best friend smokes, there is a 90 percent probability that the child will smoke too.

Likewise the Canadian Minister of National Health and Welfare, Monique Begin, told the World Conference on Smoking and Health that 'the people who most influence a child to start smoking are his or her friends and family'. This view is supported by the findings, in the same year, of Dr. M.J. Ashley of the University of Toronto, and by T.E. Moore, also of Toronto, in 1984.

Similar Findings Worldwide

These results were certainly not confined to Canada. In studies carried out in Norway in 1975 and 1980, it was shown that where both parents smoked, and permitted their children to smoke, approximately 67 per cent of the 15-year old boys and 78 per cent of girls were daily smokers. Where neither parent smoked, and the children were forbidden by parents to smoke, the comparable figures fell to 9 per cent for boys and 11 per cent for girls. Studies of British youth in 1991 and 1992 likewise found that the roles of parents and family were the keys to juvenile smoking decisions. A 1995 study published by the UK Department of Health on smoking prevalence among adolescents found that the influence of siblings was even more important than the smoking habits of parents. This same survey found that 75 per cent of adolescents who were regular smokers said that all or most of their friends smoked.

The same year, a study of smoking behaviour among more than 700 urban New Zealand children, who had been tracked from birth, found peer groups were the principal link to experimentation with smoking at age 16 or above.

Similarly, a 1988 study of Japanese youth found that an individual's smoking behaviour was 'most strongly related' to peer pressure. Likewise, a 1995 study of South Korean youth concluded that 'perceived peer use was the strongest predictor of cigarette smoking for boys and girls'.

The influence of family smoking habits was clearly revealed in a 1990 study for the Hong Kong government which concluded that youthful smoking 'is significantly related to family smoking habits'. The study noted that, in Eastern societies where much parental supervision is exercised by female family members, there was a greater disposition by youth to smoke where mothers and/or sisters also smoked. The influence of peers was held to be the principal reason for youth smoking in a 1994 study of adolescents in Australia. The study reported that:

> *"Family and friends are the major influences on smoking by the young."*

> the primary motivation to take up smoking and to keep smoking through the school years, is primarily social definition—peer identity ('where I fit in'), self-image ('who I am'), and acquiring power ('defiance /rebellion').

Smoking in American Families

Research from the United States confirms the over-riding importance of peers and family in the decision by youth to smoke. A 1995 survey of youth smoking led one researcher to say that he found it:

> 'surprising that national health lobbies and officials recently downplayed parental smoking as a promoter of youth smoking' since, in the L.A. survey, 60 per cent of young smokers 'came from the minority of the households which contained a smoking parent'.

He added that, given the universal exposure to advertising: 'it is unlikely . . . that this factor would explain much, if any, of the variance in youth smoking unexplained by parental smoking.' Thus, he concluded that, as a matter of public policy:

> the increasing politicisation of national health policies should not mislead health educators . . . [to ignore] the reality that the biggest influences on, and most accurate predictors of, youth behaviour, including smoking, remain the behaviour of parents and other adults around them.

Young people themselves invariably confirm this, as noted by a 1994 survey in Florida. One of the most interesting findings comes from the focus groups which the US Food and Drug Administration (FDA) set up in the hope of supporting further restrictions on tobacco advertising. The result was to confirm that the principal reason for starting smoking was peer pressure.

Finally, a 1991 study of 11–15-year-olds in the European Community found that across cultures there were consistent influences on smoking. The most significant influence was peer group, followed by family environment, interaction with friends, schooling and a host of other factors. Advertising was reported to play a role in smoking in only one-third of the countries surveyed and even then its influence was found to be far behind peer and family influence.

It can hardly be doubted any longer that peers and family are far and away the overwhelming reason why youths take up smoking. It is a deliberate diversion for public health officials and/or parents to attribute youth smoking to advertising.

Chapter 3

Should Smoking Be Regulated by the Government?

Chapter Preface

The health risks of smoking have led to government regulations and bans on smoking in public places in certain states. In 1998, California became the first state to ban smoking in restaurants and bars. Other states are beginning to enact similar restrictions on smoking, which has generated much controversy over whether the government has the right to limit the areas in which people can smoke.

Antismoking advocates claim that the government should protect the nonsmoking public from the dangers of secondhand smoke. Secondhand smoke, many argue, can cause the same lung cancer, emphysema, and asthma in nonsmokers as mainstream smoke can in smokers. According to Walt Bilofsky, a volunteer advocate in the area of tobacco control, "Breathing tobacco smoke can hurt anyone, but it is especially harmful to the elderly, the very young, and those with existing respiratory problems. Refraining from smoking during pregnancy and around children will give them a healthier start in life. Local smoking legislation helps make the indoor air safer in your town." Bilofsky and others argue that enacting public smoking restrictions ensures cleaner air for nonsmokers, especially vulnerable children and elderly.

Others contend that public smoking bans violate personal privacy and civil rights. Many argue that adults should have the right to smoke where they please, as they understand and accept health risks of smoking. According to author Jacob Sullum, "Secondhand smoke on private property is not imposed on people against their will. If you choose to eat in a restaurant, fly on an airplane, or work in an office where smoking is permitted, you thereby consent to exposure to secondhand smoke. You may not like it, you may even worry that it will increase your risk of getting lung cancer, but you have implicitly decided that the annoyance and the possible risks are outweighed by the benefits of eating in a particular restaurant, flying in a particular airplane, or working in a particular office." Sullum and others argue that nonsmokers are not forced to share the breathing space of smokers and should not expect the government to regulate the air quality.

Whether the government has the right to enact smoking bans is one of the issues debated in the following chapter on smoking regulations.

Tobacco Must Be Regulated by the Food and Drug Administration

by Bill Novelli

About the author: *Bill Novelli is the former president of the Campaign for Tobacco-Free Kids, a nongovernmental organization dedicated to reducing smoking among young people.*

Today more than 6,000 kids in the United States will have their first cigarette, and 3,000 or more will become new regular smokers. This happens every day of the year. If current trends continue, more than 5 million kids alive today ultimately will die from tobacco-related illnesses. Our country shouldn't let that happen.

In a major effort to reduce the terrible toll of tobacco on our children, in August 1996 then President Bill Clinton approved a new Food and Drug Administration, or FDA, rule that asserted FDA jurisdiction over tobacco and established a series of effective measures to reduce tobacco-industry marketing to kids. The FDA rule simply placed tobacco products on the same regulatory footing as other products we consume. For too long, the tobacco industry has been free to market its products, despite their deadly nature, without having to comply with many of the labeling, product-safety and other consumer-protection laws that apply to virtually all other companies—and they have taken advantage of the situation.

Incriminating Evidence

Internal industry documents reveal that for decades the tobacco industry withheld critically important information about the deadly nature of their products from consumers and the public and even lied to make them appear more safe. The industry also fully recognized the addictive power of nicotine and used that in the development and marketing of its products. FDA authority over tobacco would have prevented that kind of deceit and manipulation. Unfortunately, tobacco-company challenges to FDA's statutory authority to regulate tobacco products have blocked the implementation of everything in the FDA rule except for provisions prohibiting tobacco sales to kids younger than 18. The Supreme Court is currently considering the issue and, based on the evidence presented, should find that FDA has clear authority over tobacco products. But if the Supreme Court somehow sides with the tobacco industry, the entire FDA rule simply will disappear. Even worse, the FDA will be left with no authority to regu-

> *"Internal industry documents reveal that for decades the tobacco industry withheld critically important information about the deadly nature of their products."*

late tobacco products or marketing, and it will be business as usual for the tobacco companies. [The Supreme Court rejected the FDA tobacco legislation in March 2000.]

Unless Congress quickly remedies the situation by giving FDA explicit statutory jurisdiction over tobacco, such a ruling rejecting FDA authority would be a national tragedy. It would eliminate one of the most effective weapons that can be brought to bear against the epidemic of harmful and ultimately deadly tobacco use among our nation's children. While Congress and the states can take other effective steps to prevent and reduce tobacco use, only FDA can provide the nationwide, systematic regulation and oversight of tobacco-company activities that is necessary to minimize tobacco marketing to children, make it harder for kids to obtain tobacco products and make sure that the tobacco industry does not modify its products to be more harmful or to lure more kids into smoking.

Moreover, FDA is the only government agency that can provide comprehensive oversight of all aspects of tobacco-product development and marketing, including the companies' use of dangerous chemical additives, their nicotine manipulation and their advertising and promotional efforts that attract kids. Compared to Congress or the state legislatures, the FDA also has the ability to modify its regulations swiftly to counteract changes in tobacco-industry tactics and more effectively protect children from the hazards of tobacco use, and is less likely to be corrupted or impeded by tobacco-company money and influence.

Marketing and Advertising

Each year, U.S. tobacco companies spend more than $5 billion marketing their products. They say the marketing has no influence over kids. But studies in the *Journal of the American Medical Society,* the *Journal of the National Cancer Institute* and other medical and scientific journals say it does. Research shows that kids are three times as sensitive to tobacco advertising as adults and that roughly a third of underage experimentation with smoking is attributable to tobacco-company advertising and promotional activities. Surprising as it might sound, studies even indicate that cigarette marketing is more influential than peer pressure in getting kids to smoke. Faced with this problem, the FDA rule contains provisions that would reduce youth exposure to tobacco marketing and make the tobacco ads kids are most likely to see much less glamorous and appealing.

Similarly, the FDA rule provisions that establish and enforce a national minimum age of 18 for buying tobacco products (which are now in effect) already have made it harder for kids to obtain tobacco products. Kids still can find places to buy cigarettes, but the situation has improved dramatically. Withdrawing FDA's authority could lose these gains, and allowing the rest of the FDA rule to go into effect would make it even tougher for kids to get cigarettes.

With clear authority, FDA also could move quickly to prevent new tobacco-company efforts to market to kids. Right now, for example, there is nothing to prevent the tobacco companies from marketing their products on the Internet. The big tobacco companies have yet to take advantage of the Internet (although many smaller companies have), but that could change soon. [A] multistate settlement in 1997 banned most tobacco billboards, [and] the tobacco companies have about $250 million per year in advertising money they will want to spend elsewhere. Besides the Internet, they might also start reaching more youngsters through direct mail, which is even more difficult to police.

> *"The FDA . . . has the ability to . . . more effectively protect children from the hazards of tobacco use."*

Also, there is nothing in place right now to stop the tobacco companies from introducing new products with even more carcinogens and other poisons than current cigarettes. (Philip Morris, for example, purportedly added ammonia to Marlboros to increase their nicotine "kick.") Nor is there any legal authority to stop the marketing of flavored cigarettes, which would draw even more kids into smoking. That strategy already has worked for the spit-tobacco folks—as an industry representative said, "Cherry Skoal is for somebody who likes the taste of candy, if you know what I'm saying"—and cigarette makers could easily follow suit. In fact, industry documents show that the companies already have experimented with adding various flavorings, such as cola, that might be attractive to kids. An internal document of Brown & Williamson (makers of Kool) states, "It's a well-known fact that teenagers like sweet products. Honey might be considered." With clear authority over tobacco, FDA could ensure that these kinds of product ideas never actually appear in the marketplace.

The Tobacco Settlement

As these examples show, FDA jurisdiction over tobacco is still necessary despite the new marketing restrictions in the multistate tobacco settlement. The agreement simply is too limited and leaves too many loopholes for the industry to exploit. Its ban on billboards, for example, still allows the tobacco companies to place 14-square-foot advertisements on the outside of any store that sells tobacco products—even right next to schools.

The tobacco companies argue that further regulation is unnecessary because they have turned over a new leaf and will now act as ideal corporate citizens. Should anyone believe this? Internal industry documents reveal a long and persistent history of the tobacco industry presenting a responsible and well-intentioned face to the public in order to camouflage various forms of improper behavior. More-

> *"There is nothing in place right now to stop the tobacco companies from introducing new products with even more carcinogens and other poisons than current cigarettes."*

over, to maintain their enormous revenues and profits, the big tobacco companies have to continue attracting kids into smoking to replace adult smokers who quit or die. That's why they vigorously oppose marketing restrictions, such as those in the FDA rule, that would reduce smoking by youth but have little or no impact on their adult customers.

Some people still argue against FDA jurisdiction by raising the false specter of big government; but we are not talking about giving FDA authority over some disorganized group of small, weak businesses. This is an industry that spends more than $50 million per year lobbying the federal government (and millions more influencing state and local governments), contributes $5 million or more per year just to candidates for federal offices and has annual revenues roughly 100 times the size of the entire FDA budget. No matter how you slice it, FDA will still be a David fighting a group of politically savvy Goliaths with very deep pockets.

Free and Clear Authority

Nevertheless, with clear authority, FDA would be able to operate relatively free from political influence to analyze the tobacco problem and develop the most effective regulatory responses (as it did with the FDA rule). In contrast, leaving ongoing tobacco regulation to Congress and state legislatures means countless efforts to pass legislation over the remarkably strong political influence of the tobacco companies, often behind closed doors. Big tobacco's power to keep Congress from acting responsibly is shown by the fact that Congress failed to pass the comprehensive McCain tobacco bill in 1998, despite broad public support—and hasn't passed anything since. Leaving matters to the state legislatures offers no better hope. The tobacco companies are extremely active in every state capital. Moreover, states and localities are simply blocked by various federal laws from regulating many aspects of tobacco production and marketing.

The final argument typically made against FDA authority is that it is the first step toward a total ban on cigarettes and other tobacco products. But the FDA repeatedly has confirmed that a ban would be foolish given the extent of adult tobacco use and addiction, and it would not ban tobacco products even if it had authority to do so. More to the point, Congress has made it quite clear that it would not tolerate any ban.

As things are now, more than 400,000 people die each year from consuming tobacco products—while our regulatory system makes it harder to sell nicotine gum and nicotine patches than to market cigarettes. At the same time, more than 1 million kids a year become regular, daily smokers, while cigarettes face weaker regulatory controls than aspirin, soft drinks or breakfast cereals. That isn't fair, and it doesn't make sense. With full authority over tobacco, FDA could finally establish a more equitable regulatory framework that would rein in this industry, reduce tobacco addiction and save lives.

Government Regulation Is Necessary to Curb Youth Smoking

by John McCain

About the author: *John McCain is a Republican senator for Arizona.*

Smoking, according to the American Medical Association, is nothing less than a pediatric epidemic. Half a million Americans die of smoking-related illnesses, the vast majority of whom take up the habit in their teens.

Today, 3,000 children will begin a lifetime smoking addiction that quite likely will kill one-third of them. No fewer will begin tomorrow and every day thereafter unless we act.

These grim statistics, though staggering, can't begin to capture the human pain, suffering and loss of life they represent. Most everyone has a family member or close friend whose life ended early from a smoking-related disease. Enough is enough. The time for action is now.

Public-health authorities, including former surgeon general C. Everett Koop and past Food and Drug Administration, or FDA, head, David Kessler, agree that only a comprehensive approach to the problem of youth smoking will work.

Promising Legislation

In 1998, the Senate Commerce Committee approved the National Tobacco Policy and Youth Smoking Reduction Act by an overwhelming bipartisan vote of 19–1. The bill, modeled after the plan proposed by 40 state attorneys general in the summer of 1997, is tough medicine for a tough problem. [The bill was rejected by Congress in 1998.]

The measure was developed in cooperation with the attorneys general, representatives of the public-health sector and the Clinton administration. It contains the six major initiatives experts say must be jointly undertaken if we are to cure the pediatric epidemic of tobacco use. These elements include: (1) advertising restrictions to eliminate marketing appeals to youth; (2) higher cigarette prices to deter underage consumption; (3) aggressive youth-smoking reduction targets and industry penalties for nonattainment; (4) stronger enforcement of youth tobacco-access rules; (5) public disclosure, oversight and regulation of cigarette ingredients; and (6) industry payments to compensate for smoking-related medical costs and to finance smoking prevention, cessation and medical-research programs.

First, marketing and advertising. Documents disclosed in courts and Congress prove that tobacco companies have targeted and groomed the youth market to replace the 400,000 customers they "lose" each year. Studies show that young people are particularly susceptible to the industry's marketing pitches. So effective have these companies been at appealing to youth, that many children can identify Joe Camel as readily as they do Barney or cartoon characters.

The bill would place vast advertising and marketing restrictions on the tobacco industry, including a ban on billboards and outdoor advertising at sports arenas, as well as a prohibition of color ads and the use of human and animal figures. It would restrict point-of-sale advertising to ensure that cigarette pitches aren't directed at children and would require bold, new warning labels on cigarette packaging. And, the tobacco industry would not be permitted to pay Hollywood to have its products featured in entertainment media.

Cigarette Taxes

Second, higher cigarette prices. Experts say the most important step to deter youth consumption is to hike the price of tobacco products. Health studies show that consumption of only a modest number of cigarettes can result in clinical addiction, and that higher pricing is essential to deter underage use. Accordingly, the bill would increase the price per pack of cigarettes by a minimum of $1.10 over five years. The Clinton administration believed that this hike, included in the former president's budget request, could cut youth consumption in half.

Third, youth smoking-reduction targets. Four-and-one-half million underage Americans use tobacco, and the number is growing.

The bill calls for a 60 percent reduction in youth consumption within 10 years and levies hefty financial penalties on the tobacco industry for failing to achieve them.

Fourth, stronger enforcement of rules for youth access to tobacco products. While smoking by minors is prohibited in every state, youths continue to buy tobacco. The bill would require that tobacco products

"Most everyone has a family member or close friend whose life ended early from a smoking-related disease."

be stored in areas inaccessible to youths and required retailers to "card" tobacco purchasers in the same manner as alcohol buyers. In addition, the bill would ban vending machines, except in adult facilities, and require face-to-face transactions where teens are present.

Fifth, cigarette-ingredient regulation. Cigarettes contain numerous active ingredients harmful to health, including nicotine, tar and ammonia. Evidence suggests that the tobacco industry has manipulated these ingredients to enhance their addictive qualities and, in some instances, added benign substances such as molasses to sweeten the taste for introductory users—our children.

The bill would permit the FDA to oversee and regulate tobacco products in order to protect public health and promote the development of safer cigarettes. . . . Moreover, the FDA would have to consider the black-market potential of any modification to cigarettes that would push users to seek contraband products.

Healthcare Costs

Sixth, industry payments. Smoking-related health-care costs exceed a whopping $45 billion per year! The bill would require the industry to pay $516 billion during the next 25 years to reimburse taxpayers for costs to Medicare and state healthcare programs. These funds also would be employed to finance smoking-related health research, prevention and cessation activities, as well as to help innocent tobacco farmers and rural communities affected by changes in the industry.

Finally, the bill would place a cap on the tobacco industry's exposure to legal liability without barring any individual or group's ability to sue or receive compensation. The tobacco industry has successfully fended off

> *"Many children can identify Joe Camel as readily as they do Barney or cartoon characters."*

lawsuits for years. However, should trends change and massive new judgments be awarded against the tobacco industry, bankruptcy is always a possibility. [The 1998 Master Settlement Agreement resolved lawsuits aimed at recovering the medical costs of treating smokers from the tobacco companies.]

Experts agree that bankruptcy is an undesirable outcome for the nation economically, legally and medically. Involving bankruptcy would permit the industry to shield itself from its financial responsibilities, including compensation to victims. When the asbestos companies went bankrupt and left the financial and legal mess that is still with us, only the lawyers made out. Moreover, the extinction of domestic manufacturers would simply push tobacco users to purchase foreign brands or unregulated contraband which would lead to a public-health crisis.

Legal Challenges

We have heard many opinions about whether the industry—at the end of the day—will submit to this legislation. Legal challenges, of course, would delay reforms, so industry cooperation would be advantageous. While public-health authorities insist that price hikes are the key to cutting underage smoking, they alone won't do the job.

The proposed advertising restrictions and youth-usage penalties, which the industry is threatening to challenge, are essential pieces of the puzzle.

The National Tobacco Policy and Youth Smoking Reduction Act, however, was never intended to be a "deal" with the tobacco industry. Our mission was to pass the best possible legislation to stop youth smoking. . . .

Tobacco is a legal product and the decision to use it, though risky, is a choice for adults to make. Nevertheless, the nation requires that the tobacco industry join us in the fight to protect our children. If they choose not to, the American people will respond accordingly. Congress will act, and the states will resume their lawsuits to extract in court what we might more efficiently achieve through cooperation.

The real bottom line for tobacco legislation is not about the industry's finances but rather, the health of our children.

The Government Should Not Regulate Smoking

by the *Economist*

About the author: *The* Economist *is a weekly international news and business publication that focuses on such issues as business, finance, science and technology, books, and culture.*

Tobacco is not, properly speaking, a social problem at all, but the growing anti-smoking movement is quickly becoming one.

One began to suspect that the attack on smoking in America—the industrial world's leading moral exporter—was escalating rather out of hand when in 1996 the attorney general of Texas announced, apparently in all seriousness, that "history will record the modern-day tobacco industry alongside the worst of civilisation's evil empires"; when a *New York Times* book reviewer suggested that "only slavery exceeds tobacco as a curse on American history"; when an anti-tobacco activist and plaintiff called tobacco firms "the most criminal, disgusting, sadistic, degenerate group of people on the face of the earth." Not long ago an earnest young American assured the *Economist* that breathing other people's smoke is morally equivalent to being sprayed with machine-gun fire. Your correspondent (a non-smoker) was reduced to an undignified gape.

The *Economist* is all in favour of the occasional moral crusade, provided popcorn is sold. Certainly, smoking is a messy and short-sighted habit, and tobacco companies are not particularly nice. Lately, however, the attack on tobacco has crossed the admittedly fuzzy line that distinguishes moral enthusiasm from illiberal vindictiveness, and at such a time good fun should yield to good thinking. Most people in America and Europe would agree, without a second thought, that smoking is a public health problem. But is this really so?

Smoking undoubtedly warrants some modest public measures, most of which have already been taken in the industrialised countries: moderate tobacco taxes, public education, and prevention of unreasonable nuisance to non-smokers. But smoking is not like tuberculosis or air pollution or drunken driving; it is not, strictly speaking, a public-health or public-safety problem at all. Rather, like motorcycling or overeating or skiing, it is a private health problem. To be specific, it is a problem for smokers. In seeking to obliterate this point, the anti-smoking crusade is in imminent danger of becoming a campaign against liberal principles, which is to say, a campaign of intolerance. It is time for a rethink from first premises. The argument that follows focuses primarily on America, where anti-smoking fervour has reached a high pitch; but the principles apply everywhere.

Privacy and Puffery

In 1690, John Locke remade society with a revolutionary claim, which was that just because something may improve people's lives does not give a government the proper authority to do it. Undoubtedly, he said, it is good for people to believe in the true religion (the Church of England, of course); but the magistrate, he added, nonetheless "has no commission, no right," to enforce proper piety. The point he was making is the foundation-stone of toleration in particular and of liberal government in general: that there is a private sphere which governments may not invade, even for the obvious benefit of those affected. A goodly share of today's anti-smoking rhetoric is crafted to fudge this principle, or to drown it out with indignant noise.

To be a problem for somebody, an act need only be problematic. But to be a problem for society—a public concern, as liberalism would define one—it must either harm unconsenting people or entail perils which the practitioner himself cannot reasonably understand and avoid. Moreover, governments cannot regulate even harmful behaviour wantonly, but must settle for the narrowest restrictions that alleviate the harm or protect potential victims. Once government has punished drunken drivers and publicised the hazards of drink, it should not go on to ban alcohol or require distillers to pay for new public hospitals.

To turn smoking into a public-health crusade, then, anti-smokers need to do more than say that smoking is stupid and that fewer people should do it. So they respond with a string of claims intended to drag smoking into the realm of public authority. None is strong.

To begin with, they note that smoking is a needless and common cause of illness and death. But by itself this proves nothing. People take such risks all the time. Motorcycling is about 16 times more dangerous than driving a car; but a motorcyclist will

> *"Smoking is not like tuberculosis or air pollution or drunken driving; it is not . . . a public-health or public-safety problem."*

tell you that the pleasure of wind in the hair and a powerful engine between the thighs is worth the risk. Smoking, which can both soothe and stimulate, entails just the same sort of risk-for-pleasure trade.

The public-health rhetoric often implies that smoking must be daft, because it is deadly. In fact, most smokers (two-thirds or more) do not die of smoking-related disease. They gamble and win. Moreover, the years lost to smoking come from the end of life, when people are most likely to die of something else anyway. Former president Bill Clinton's mother, who died of cancer at the age of 70 after smoking two packs a day for most of her life, might, as Mr. Clinton notes, have extended her life by not smoking; but she might also have extended it by eating better or exercising more, and in any case she could never have been sure. From a moral point of view smoking is a lot like eating a fatty diet (and note that sticking to a rigorous low-fat diet is at least as hard as quitting nicotine). Smoking may deserve friendly criticism, but it does not warrant moral indignation, any more than skiing does, and no more is it anyone else's affair.

Those Fatal Fumes

Ah, but what if non-smokers are involuntarily exposed to wafting clouds of ghastly gas? Anti-smokers understandably rush to emphasise the risks of so-called passive smoking, or external tobacco smoke. But second-hand smoke is less helpful to them than they believe.

For one thing, they commonly exaggerate its dangers, or, to be more precise, they exaggerate the extent to which it is known to do much harm at all. In 1995, America's Congressional Research Service noted that only seven of the 34 studies then available found statistically significant health effects from passive smoking, and one of those found that the effect is positive—ie, that passive smoking is good for you. Of course, it is not really good for

> *"To turn smoking into a public-health crusade, . . . anti-smokers need to do more than say that smoking is stupid and that fewer people should do it."*

you: the real point is that its effects are so small as to be hard to pin down with any certainty at all. Moreover, to find consistently measurable effects, you have to study spouses who live day in and day out with a heavy smoker for many years, something that adults presumably do more or less voluntarily. Evidence of medical harm from the stray wisp of smoke in a workplace or restaurant remains vanishingly thin.

However, let us grant that second-hand smoke is probably a small health hazard; in any case, it is certainly a smelly nuisance. Here the solution is obvious: where people object to smoke, restrict smoking to unbothersome places. With the possible exception of children and spouses of smokers (who put up with each other's offensive habits of every sort, and presumably are best left to sort out such problems among themselves), segregating smokers wholly solves the passive-smoke problem. In America and increasingly in Europe, smoking is commonly restricted to separate areas. End of problem.

Anti-smokers have become fond of arguing that nothing short of a total ban on smoking in all places of work will do, since separate smoking areas still leave some workers, such as waiters and bartenders, exposed to fumes. But it is not reasonable to demand that every risk or inconvenience be eliminated from every workplace or public area, for that is an unending and ultimately quite radical project. Some drinkers will choose to patronise smoky bars, and some bartenders will be glad to work there. This should be allowed.

Anti-smokers next point out that smokers cost society money. Smokers use publicly financed medical care, they take leave for illness, they burn down the odd building. Surely they should pay for the costs they incur.

> *"The solution is obvious: where people object to smoke, restrict smoking to unbothersome places."*

They do. Several economic analyses have been done, says Kip Viscusi, a Harvard University economist, "and they all show that smokers save society money." Smokers die before they can collect their expensive public pensions and nursing-home benefits. Moreover, cigarettes are the world's most heavily taxed consumer good. In America, which is on the low side by industrial-country standards, the tax has averaged $ 0.57 a pack (varying by state, and rose 10 cents on January 1, 1998). This is more than is needed to pay what anybody thinks smokers cost society, even when you include a generous estimate for the social costs of second-hand smoke.

Forced to Smoke?

Let there be no uncertainty about what is going on here: smokers are paying the rest of us for the privilege of puffing. The rest of us may justify this on grounds that smoking less would be better for smokers. But why not, then, a fatty-foods tax? A motorcycle tax? A failure-to-floss tax? If anyone is being treated unfairly in the current scheme, it is the smokers. In any event, once smokers pay their own way, which they more than do already, monetary cost provides no excuse to treat smoking as the public's business.

Bereft of better grounds to assert that smoking is a social problem, anti-smoking activists then become creative. Some of them assert, for instance, that parents' smoking hurts asthmatic children. This may be true, but it is an argument for better parents, not fewer cigarettes. More commonly, some crusaders argue that smokers are pawns of tobacco companies, which ought to be punished.

On this line, one American anti-smoking activist says that cigarette makers are "responsible for the premature deaths of more Americans than any other group of individuals who have ever lived"; a British headline declares "Cigarette makers ready to buy off their victims"; a prominent anti-tobacco lawyer likens tobacco companies to "the bully who physically assaults a victim unable to defend himself." It is impressive how common this sort of sentiment has become, given that, on its face, the portrayal of smokers as bullied or deceived victims is preposterous.

Tobacco companies should not have been expected to declare cigarettes poisonous before that fact became firmly established; and when it did become established, it was promptly plastered, in plain language, on every tobacco advert and cigarette package, and shouted from every public-health rooftop. Big Tobacco's subsequent refusal to acknowledge that smoking is harmful or habit-forming may have been duplicitous, but it surely scores as the most spectacularly unsuccessful disinformation campaign in history, since anyone who does not know that smoking is bad for you lives on Mars.

Coffin Nails

Even before science established definitively that tobacco can kill you, people knew it was trouble. In America, cigarettes have been referred to as "coffin nails" for more than a century. Franklin Roosevelt once joked to a boy that he used the cigarette holder "because my doctor told me to stay as far away from cigarettes as possible." By the 1950s, surveys found that the overwhelming majority of people (90%, in a 1954 Gallup poll), old and young, had heard that cigarettes can cause cancer.

Since then, public education about smoking has been a rousing success: since 1965, a year after the first definitive health warning, the rate of smoking in America has declined from more than 40% to about 25%, and the number of ex-smokers has trebled. Surveys show that by now the public, including smokers themselves, have a greatly exaggerated notion of smoking's peril; Mr. Viscusi, for instance, has found that the chances of getting cancer from cigarettes are typically overstated by a multiple of four or more. Plainly people have been duly informed. If they continue to smoke, that is not because anyone has fooled them.

It is true that tobacco advertising glamorises tobacco, which is dangerous. It is also true that motorcycle advertising glamorises motorcycles, which are dangerous. Both types of advert are arguably unwholesome, but the notion that a demonstrably well-informed public is helpless to resist them is silly, as much research has found.

"There is no clear relationship between restrictions on tobacco advertising and consumption of tobacco," says Jacob Sullum, the author of *For Your Own Good: The Anti-Smoking Crusade and the Tyranny of Public Health. . . .* In countries that have banned tobacco advertising, cigarette consumption has not been affected in any consistent way. A 1993 study of 22 countries found no statistically significant effect from bans on tobacco advertising, and the insignificant effect was to increase consumption slightly. This is not so surprising, since tobacco adverts carry health warnings. Not even among youths is advertising demonstrably important, or a ban on adverts demonstrably helpful; a lorry-load of research finds, as with adults, no systematic relationship.

> *"Smokers are paying the rest of us for the privilege of puffing."*

Addictive Arguments

Here, however, the enemies of smoking lay down what they regard as a trump card. Smoking, unlike motorcycling, is addictive. And that is true. Nicotine quickly establishes a strong physical craving enforced by withdrawal pains (apparently by exploiting some of the same neural pathways as cocaine and opiates). But nicotine is not impossible to quit, merely difficult. There are today as many people who have quit smoking as there are people who smoke. Mr. Sullum points out, America's National Survey on Drug Abuse finds that almost three-fourths of respondents had tried smoking, but only about 30% had smoked in the past month. This can hardly be a substance that demolishes the will.

Philosophically speaking, to take up smoking is merely to make a risky decision which is hard to reverse. People make risky, hard-to-reverse decisions all the time: marrying a violent man, donating a kidney, joining a cult, gambling their savings. If adulthood means anything, it means being able to choose a risky path even if turning back is difficult, provided that one is fully informed; and people are at least as well aware that smoking is hard to quit as that it is bad for you. Addictiveness, then, is biologically interesting, but it does not make a "social" problem of smoking. It does not even make a special problem of smoking.

> *"There is no clear relationship between restrictions on tobacco advertising and consumption of tobacco."*

One last argument is left, ever the final redoubt of illiberalism: protection of the young. Surely cigarette advertising and availability tempt those whose judgment is weakest. After all, the vast majority of smokers (90% or more) start as teenagers.

There is something in this argument, but less than enough to justify all that missionaries would do in its name. Adolescent bravado and myopia may indeed justify limiting smoking—like driving, voting and marrying—to adults; and such restrictions on the rights of children are fully consistent with liberalism. Most places forbid or regulate the sale of cigarettes to the young, and this is appropriate.

Sanitising Advertisements

If youths are less wise than their elders, however, that is true in every department of life, and it gives no reason to hound adults. If the glamorisation of unhealthful habits is to be forbidden, then why stop with smoking adverts when ice cream, motorbikes, and suntans pose so much risk? Sanitising advertising for the sake of children is no more defensible than sanitising films or censoring the Internet for their sake; harassing smokers in the name of children's welfare is no more defensible than harassing homosexuals or socialists.

Even such justifiable measures as education and bans on sales to the young should not be pushed too far. To tell a teenager that some practice is too dangerous for children is to beg him to embrace it. In the state of Massachusetts, teen-age smoking rose 10% after an aggressive anti-smoking campaign began; since 1992 teenage smoking has risen in America even as the overall rate has fallen, a fact that anti-smoking hysteria may partly explain. It is best, on the whole, to make sure the young understand the dangers of smoking—as they assuredly do, for they exaggerate the perils of tobacco even more than adults do—and then let parents encourage sensible behaviour as best they can. That is done already, and has been for years.

> *"Harassing smokers in the name of children's welfare is no more defensible than harassing homosexuals or socialists."*

In 1996, the parliament of Iran approved a ban on smoking in any public place. In Iran, however, the ban was soon overturned as being, of all things, unconstitutional. Meanwhile, under a law passed in the state of California on January 1, 1998 it became illegal to smoke in any bar, even if (as in "cigar bars") customers, proprietors and employees willingly seek solace in tobacco fumes. Surely something is wrong with this picture.

Because they are nursing their dudgeon and savouring their victories rather than thinking with care, anti-smokers believe themselves to be upholding liberal social principles when in fact they are traducing them. That is both ironic and unfortunate. Establishing Locke's principle—the demarcation of a privileged private sphere, where even well-intentioned snoops may not go—was the work of centuries. It should not be relinquished in a puff of smoke.

Government Regulation of Smoking Is an Attempt to Control the Public

by Robert H. Bork

About the author: *Robert H. Bork is a John M. Olin scholar at the American Enterprise Institute, a conservative public-policy research organization in Washington, D.C.*

Government efforts to deal with tobacco companies betray an ultimate ambition to control Americans' lives.

When moral self-righteousness, greed for money, and political ambition work hand in hand they produce irrational, but almost irresistible, policies. The latest example is the war on cigarettes and cigarette smokers. A proposed settlement was negotiated in 1997 among politicians, plaintiffs' lawyers, and the tobacco industry. The only interests left out of the negotiations were smokers', who will be ordered to pay enormous sums with no return other than the deprivation of their own choices and pleasures.

It is a myth that today's Americans are a sturdy, self-reliant folk who will fight any officious interference with their liberties. That has not been true at least since the New Deal. If you doubt that, walk the streets of any American city and see the forlorn men and women cupping their hands against the wind to light cigarettes so that they can get through a few more smokeless hours in their offices. Twenty-five per cent of Americans smoke. Why can't they demand and get a compromise rather than accepting docilely the exile that employers and building managers impose upon them?

The answer is that they have been made to feel guilty by self-righteous non-smokers. A few years back, hardly anyone claimed to be seriously troubled by tobacco smoke. Now, an entire class of the morally superior claim to be able to detect, and be offended by, tobacco smoke several offices away from their own. These people must possess the sense of smell of a deer or an Indian guide. Yet they will happily walk through suffocating exhaust smoke from buses rather than wait a minute or two to cross the street.

Health Fanaticism

No one should assume that peace will be restored when the last cigarette smoker has been banished to the Alaskan tundra. Other products will be pressed into service as morally reprehensible. If you would know the future, look to California—the national leader in health fanaticism. After a long day in Los Angeles flogging a book I had written, my wife and I sought relaxation with a drink at our hotel's outdoor bar. Our anticipation of pleasure was considerably diminished by a sign: "Warning! Toxic Substances Served Here." They were talking about my martini!

And martinis are a toxic substance, taken in any quantity sufficient to induce a sense of well-being. Why not, then, ban alcohol or at least require a death's head on every martini glass? Well, we did once outlaw alcohol; it was called Prohibition. The myth is that Prohibition increased the amount of drinking in this country; the truth is that it reduced it. There were, of course, some unfortunate side effects, like Al Capone and Dutch Schultz. But by and large the mobsters inflicted rigor mortis upon one another.

Why is it, then, that the end of Prohibition was welcomed joyously by the population? Not because alcohol is not dangerous. Not because the consumption of alcohol was not lessened. And not in order to save the lives of people with names like Big Jim and Ice Pick Phil. Prohibition came to an end because most Americans wanted to have a drink when and where they felt like it. If you insist on sounding like a law-and-economics professor, it ended because we thought the benefits of alcohol outweighed the costs.

Benefits vs. Costs

That is the sort of calculation by which we lead our lives. Automobiles kill tens of thousands of people every year and disable perhaps that many again. We could easily stop the slaughter. Cars could be made with a top speed of ten miles an hour and with exteriors the consistency of marshmallows. Nobody would die, nobody would be disabled, and nobody would bother with cars very much.

"Why can't [smokers] demand and get a compromise rather than accepting docilely the exile that employers and building managers impose upon them?"

There are, of course, less draconian measures available. On most highways, it is almost impossible to find anyone who observes the speed limits. On the theory of the tobacco precedent, car manufacturers should be liable for deaths caused by speeding; after all, they could build automobiles incapable of exceeding legal speed limits.

The reason we are willing to offer up lives and limbs to automobiles is, quite simply, that they make life more pleasant (for those who remain intact)— among other things, by speeding commuting to work, by making possible family vacations a thousand miles from home, and by lowering the costs of products shipped from a distance. The case for regulating automobiles far more severely than we do is not essentially different from the case for heavy regulation of cigarettes or, soon, alcohol.

But choices concerning driving, smoking, and drinking are the sort of things that ought to be left to the individual unless there are clear, serious harms to others.

In the Name of the Children

The opening salvo in the drive to make smoking a criminal act is the 1997 settlement among the cigarette companies, plaintiffs' lawyers, and the states' attorneys general. We are told that the object is to protect teenagers and children (children being the last refuge of the sanctimonious). But many restrictions will necessarily affect adults, and the tobacco pact contains provisions that can only be explained as punishment for selling to adults.

The terms of the settlement plainly reveal an intense hatred of smoking. Opposition to the pact comes primarily from those who think it is not severe enough. For example, critics say the settlement is defective in not restricting the marketing of cigarettes overseas by American tobacco companies. Connecticut's attorney general, Richard Blumenthal, defended the absence of such a provision: "Given our druthers we would have brought them to their knees all over the world, but there is a limit to our leverage." So much for the sovereignty of nations.

What the settlement does contain is bad enough. The pact would require the companies to pony up $60 billion; $25 billion of this would be used for public-health issues to be identified by a presidential panel and the rest for children's health insurance. Though the purpose of the entire agreement is punitive, this slice is most obviously so.

The industry is also required to pay $308 billion over 25 years, in part to repay states for the cost of treating sick smokers. There are no grounds for this provision. The tobacco companies have regularly won litigation against plaintiffs claiming injury on the grounds that everybody has known for the past forty years that smoking can cause health problems. This $308 billion, which takes from the companies what they have won in litigation, says, in effect, that no one assumed the risk of his own behavior.

Money-Saving Smokers

The provision is groundless for additional reasons. The notion that the states have lost money because of cigarettes ignores the federal and state taxes smokers have paid, which cover any amount the states could claim to have lost. Furthermore, a percentage of the population dies early from smoking. Had these people lived longer, the drain on Medicare and Medicaid would have been greater. When lowered pension and Social Security costs are figured in, it seems certain that government is better off financially with smoking than without it. If we must reduce the issue to one of dollars, as the attorneys general have done, states have profited financially from smoking. If this seems a gruesome and heartless calculation, it is. But don't blame me. The state governments advanced the financial argument and ought to live with its consequences, however distasteful.

Other provisions of the settlement fare no better under the application of common sense. The industry is to reduce smoking by teenagers by 30 per cent by 2002, 50 per cent by 2004, and 60 per cent by 2007. No one knows how the industry is to perform this trick. But if those goals are not met, the industry will be amerced $80 million a year for each percentage point it falls short.

> *"On the theory of the tobacco precedent, car manufacturers should be liable for deaths caused by speeding."*

The settlement assumes teenage smoking can be reduced dramatically by requiring the industry to conduct an expensive anti-smoking advertising campaign, banning the use of people and cartoon characters to promote cigarettes, and similar tactics. It is entirely predictable that this will not work. Other countries have banned cigarette advertising, only to watch smoking increase. Apparently the young, feeling themselves invulnerable, relish the risk of smoking. Studies have shown, moreover, that teenagers are drawn to smoking not because of advertising but because their parents smoke or because of peer pressure. Companies advertise to gain or maintain market share among those who already smoke.

To lessen the heat on politicians, the pact increases the powers of the Food and Drug Administration (FDA) to regulate tobacco as an addictive drug, with the caveat that it may not prohibit cigarette smoking altogether before the year 2009. The implicit promise is that the complete prohibition of cigarettes will be seriously contemplated at that time. In the meantime, the FDA will subject cigarettes to stricter and stricter controls on the theory that tobacco is a drug.

Another rationale for prohibiting or sharply limiting smoking is the supposed need to protect non-smokers from secondhand smoke. The difficulty is that evidence of causation is weak. What we see is a possible small increase in an already small risk which, as some researchers have pointed out, may well be caused by other variables such as misclassification of former smokers as non-smokers or such lifestyle factors as diet.

But the tobacco companies should take little or no comfort from that. Given today's product-liability craze, scientific support, much less probability, is unnecessary to successful lawsuits against large corporations.

Violating Free Speech?

The pact is of dubious constitutionality as well. It outlaws the advertising of a product it is legal to sell, which raises the problem of commercial speech protected by the First Amendment. The settlement also requires the industry to disband its lobbying organization, the Tobacco Institute. Lobbying has traditionally been thought to fall within the First Amendment's guarantee of the right to petition the government for the redress of grievances.

And who is to pay for making smoking more difficult? Smokers will have the price of cigarettes raised by new taxes and by the tobacco companies' costs of complying with the settlement. It is a brilliant strategy: Smokers will pay billions to have their pleasure taken away.

But if the tobacco settlement makes little sense as public policy, what can be driving it to completion? The motivations are diverse. Members of the plaintiffs' bar . . . are to be guaranteed billions of dollars annually. The states' attorneys general have a different set of incentives. They are members of the National Association of Attorneys General, NAAG, which is commonly, and accurately, rendered as the National Association of Aspiring Governors.

So far they have got what they wanted. There they are, on the front pages of newspapers all over the country, looking out at us, jaws firm, conveying images of sobriety, courage, and righteousness. They have, after all, done battle with the forces of evil, and won—at least temporarily.

Tobacco executives and their lawyers are said to be wily folk, however. They may find ways of defeating the strictures laid upon them. It may be too soon to tell, therefore, whether the tobacco settlement is a major defeat or a victory for the industry. In any case, we can live with it. But whenever individual responsibility is denied, government control of our behavior follows. After cigarettes it will be something else, and so on ad infinitum. One would think we would have learned that lesson many times over and that we would have had enough of it.

Taxing Cigarettes Unfairly Targets the Poor

by Jonathan Chait

About the author: *Jonathan Chait is a senior editor at* The New Republic, *a weekly political journal.*

When the Democratic leaders of Congress sat down with President [George H.W.] Bush in 1990 to hammer out a budget agreement, they insisted that the deal not impose any additional tax burdens on the poor. After every new twist in the negotiations, the conferees would pause as their staff economists compiled tables detailing how each income category would fare under any given combination of taxes. And although the final agreement did include higher "sin taxes" on cigarettes and liquor—which hit low-income taxpayers disproportionately— the Democrats insisted that this regressive burden be offset by an expansion of the earned income tax credit, a subsidy for the working poor.

This concern with distributional equity was very much in keeping with the Democratic Party's historic role as protector of the economic underdog. Now, however, something very different is happening. The Democratic Party, with the help of some Republicans, has decided to tax the dickens out of cigarettes.

Since everybody seems to have forgotten, let's refresh our memories about who pays cigarette taxes. Any sales levy that exacts the same tax from all comers, regardless of ability to pay, is inherently regressive. A sales tax on bread, for example, would exact a relatively higher toll on the poor than on the wealthy, because the poor must spend a higher percentage of their income on food. A cigarette tax is even more regressive than a bread tax, because the poor tend to smoke more heavily than the wealthy. Adding $1.50 to the cost of a pack of cigarettes would cost taxpayers who earn less than $10,000 per year four percent of their income; by contrast, it would cost those earning more than $200,000 per year just one-tenth of a percent of their income, according to Citizens for Tax Justice, a liberal tax-research group.

Class Ramifications

Ordinarily, such punishment of the lower classes would evoke stirring denunciations from the [Democrats] of the world. Yet nothing of the sort has happened. On the contrary, liberal Democrats are championing cigarette taxes far larger than the ones they grudgingly and conditionally acceded to in 1990, and they have made no effort to counterbalance the huge costs such a tax will impose upon the poor. Indeed, they have blithely shrugged off the clear class ramifications of taxing tobacco and, with barely a word of protest, proceeded headlong toward a dubious experiment in government paternalism. Conservatives with ties to the tobacco industry—who are practically the only ones speaking out against this effort—have lambasted this proposal as liberalism run amok, but it would be better described as liberalism betrayed.

Why are the Democrats so eager to soak the poor? The obvious and conventional explanation is the lure of easy financing for new spending programs. Under the current budgetary rules, you must find a source of funding for any new spending initiative. That is, any new spending must be offset by equally large spending cuts or tax increases. In practice, this means that any new spending cannot pass without upsetting some political constituency. But opinion polls show that the public approves of taxing tobacco. Thus, a tobacco tax would provide Democrats with a politically easy way to finance their new domestic agenda.

Former President Bill Clinton pointed to the prospect of new spending as a justification for the regressivity of the cigarette tax. Democrats have made just this kind of bargain before. Social Security is financed by a regressive payroll tax, yet Social Security distributes its benefits progressively enough that low-wage workers still get a good deal. The cigarette tax could pass the fairness test if the White House could devote the revenues toward sufficiently munificent ends. For example, if the money coming in through the tobacco tax went back out primarily as subsidies to provide universal health coverage, day care for parents on workfare, or an expansion of the earned income tax credit, liberals could justify it as part of a progressive bargain.

But that's not how the money will be spent. [The White House] would spend about one-third of the tobacco money on anti-smoking programs, compensation for tobacco farmers, and unrestricted funding for state governments (as promised under the tobacco settlement). Of the remaining two-thirds,

> *"The Democratic Party . . . has decided to tax the dickens out of cigarettes."*

the lion's share would go toward increased funding for medical and scientific research—a worthy expenditure, to be sure, but not one that would disproportionately benefit low-income groups. Less than one-quarter of the cigarette-tax revenues remain for programs that mainly help the less prosperous. . . .

Republicans insist that any cigarette-tax revenues should pay for other tax cuts. And the tax cuts they propose—correcting the "marriage penalty" or giving tax deductions to people who buy their own health insurance—are all skewed heavily in favor of upper-income groups. In fact, devoting the cigarette-tax revenues to GOP-favored tax cuts might be the only way to win conservative support for a tobacco settlement. "If I could ensure that, every dime of a tobacco tax increase would go towards a tax cut, I might support it," wrote House Whip Tom DeLay in a 1998 *Wall Street Journal* op-ed. (This is why Republican complaints about the regressivity of the cigarette tax should be taken with a grain of salt; their true fear isn't that the tax is too regressive but that the revenues from it won't be spent regressively enough.) In any event, the final product of any tobacco deal approved by Congress will likely raise taxes at the bottom of the income scale and lower them at the top.

To the White House—and other supporters of the bill—these distributional consequences of higher cigarette prices are unpleasant but rather beside the point. "It's more complicated than a tax distribution table," says Clinton adviser Bruce Reed. "The reason we're for the price increase is that it's the most important step to keep young people from starting in the first place." [The tax increase on cigarettes was rejected by the Senate in 1998.]

The premise that higher cigarette prices will dramatically reduce youth smoking certainly makes intuitive sense—in an efficient market, raising the price for a product will lower demand for it. And the administration's theory is, in fact, supported by a con-

> *"Liberal[s] . . . have made no effort to counterbalance the huge costs . . . a [cigarette] tax will impose upon the poor."*

siderable body of research. Nonetheless, it is a much less certain proposition than the White House and its allies make it out to be.

The relevant factor in this matter is "elasticity," which is an economics term that describes how much a given kind of behavior can change in response to incentives. Behavior that is apt to change is elastic. Rigid behavior is inelastic. The question of whether taxes can keep kids away from cigarettes, then, boils down to whether or not teenagers' demand for cigarettes is elastic—i.e., whether or not a rise in the price of cigarettes will cause the demand for them to drop. If teen cigarette demand is elastic, a cigarette tax could reduce youth smoking. If it is inelastic, then a tax won't work.

Studies have shown that states with higher cigarette taxes have lower rates of teen smoking. Thus, researchers have long deduced that the demand for cigarettes among youths is elastic. In other words, higher taxes raise the cost of smoking and cause the youth-smoking rate to drop. The standard explanation for this is that, since teens are not yet addicted to nicotine, and since they don't have much money, higher cigarette prices will discourage them from buying cigarettes.

Researchers at Cornell University, however, identified a common flaw in all these findings: States with high cigarette taxes also tend to be the ones with strong anti-smoking sentiment. States where the public approves of smoking, on the other hand, do not institute high taxes on cigarettes in the first place. If this is true, then cigarette taxes are not the independent variable that determines whether or not teens smoke. Instead, a third factor—general attitudes toward smoking—is determining both the level of taxation and the level of teen smoking.

> *"The final product of any tobacco deal approved by Congress will likely raise taxes at the bottom of the income scale and lower them at the top."*

For instance, the major tobacco-producing states—North Carolina, Kentucky, and Virginia—have the lowest cigarette taxes in the country, and eighth-graders in these states also smoke more than their counterparts elsewhere. Conventional thinking would interpret this fact as yet more evidence that low cigarette taxes cause more teen smoking. But it's entirely possible that the reason kids in these states smoke more than kids in other states is simply that people in North Carolina, Kentucky, and Virginia are more tolerant of smoking. This tolerance also explains why these states have low cigarette taxes: People don't dislike smoking as much, so they don't want to tax it as much. Not only that: State governments want to do everything they can to protect demand for the local tobacco farmer's crop.

Sure enough, when the Cornell researchers examined the relationship between cigarette prices and youth smoking in every state except North Carolina, Kentucky, and Virginia, the elasticity disappeared. Kids in the remaining low-tax states were not more or less likely to smoke than the kids in high-tax states. Hence, the study found, raising the cigarette tax would not do very much to curtail youth smoking.

This explanation makes sense once you think about how and why teenagers start smoking in the first place. Teen smoking is a matter of youth culture more than youth economics. Kids start smoking because of peer pressure, and most of them smoke, at most, just a few dozen cigarettes a week with their friends. Since each cigarette costs only about a dime, smoking doesn't put much strain on a typical teenager's budget—and it still wouldn't, even if government raises the price of each cigarette by another nickel. How many teenagers, after all, would be willing to risk their social standing to save a few bucks a week?

The Cornell study was not the first to cast doubt on the notion that cigarette taxes can dissuade kids from smoking. But it was the first to highlight the flawed assumptions of the studies that suggest otherwise. As researchers have looked more closely at youth smoking, they have generally grown less certain that taxes can keep kids from smoking. "Gradually, the elasticities have fallen," observes Jane Gravelle, an economist with the nonpartisan Congressional Research Service.

New Justifications

Given that the smoking propensities of youths remain mysterious, it seems strange to tax the 98 percent of smokers who are adults in order to experiment on the two percent of smokers who aren't. Here we arrive at the philosophical crux of the Democrats' position. The White House believes higher cigarette prices will induce some adult smokers to quit and others to smoke less heavily, thereby improving their health.

This is an altogether new kind of justification for regulating cigarettes. It is not like banning smoking in the workplace, which protects nonsmokers from being forced to breathe in their coworkers' secondhand smoke. Nor is it like restricting tobacco advertising, which protects children (who cannot always make informed decisions) from a dangerous product. Rather, the intent is to protect adult smokers from themselves. As a Treasury Department official concedes: "Quite frankly, we're making a paternalistic argument because it's an addictive product."

The claim here is simple. Since nicotine is addictive, adult smokers cannot rationally choose how much they smoke. For purposes of the decision whether or not to smoke, they are, in effect, children. Therefore, the government will try to induce them to quit for their own good. "Our view is that smoking is a regressive habit," argues Reed. The poor will pay more taxes, the Treasury Department official acknowledges, but they "will gain disproportionately in health terms."

But there's a paradox. The people gaining in health terms aren't exactly the same people who pay the tax. Those who enjoy the most health benefits—the ones who reduce their smoking—will pay the least tax. Those who continue their smoking habit will get no health benefits at all but will pay the most tax. The minimum-wage worker who spends another five percent of his income on tobacco taxes will hardly be comforted by the knowledge that his neighbor who quit has added another couple of years to his life expectancy.

> *"General attitudes toward smoking . . . [determine] both the level of taxation and the level of teen smoking."*

Second, the [Democrats] are having it both ways about addiction. The addictiveness of smoking may offer a rationale for protecting smokers from themselves, but it undercuts the rationale for taxing them. Why punish people for behavior they can't control?

Smokers Can Quit

The overriding problem with paternalism is that it overstates the meaning of addiction. Nicotine may be addictive, but that doesn't mean smokers have lost all free will. One-half of all adults who have ever smoked have quit. As Harvard law professor W. Kip Viscusi shows in *Smoking: Making the Risky Decision*, smokers fully comprehend the health risks of cigarettes. Viscusi conducted surveys about the probability that cigarettes could cause lung cancer, for instance, and found that a large majority of the public overstates the risk of contracting lung cancer from smoking. Smoking, then, is not quite a fully rational decision to trade health and longevity for the pleasure of tobacco, but neither is it a purely compulsive tic of the helpless addict.

The tobacco industry has cheapened the language of individual freedom. But, in the end, smoking really is largely a personal decision. It's fine to regulate cigarette advertising or to protect nonsmokers from secondhand smoke. These activities have broad effects. Liberalism also holds, however, that individuals should be able to make their own decisions on matters that only affect themselves. The hard choices come when the demands of economic justice and personal liberty collide. On the matter of cigarette taxes, the two values dovetail. How did liberals wind up on the other side?

Chapter 4

How Can Smoking Be Reduced?

CURRENT CONTROVERSIES

Chapter Preface

Quitting smoking is extremely difficult for most people—many heroin addicts who smoke claim that nicotine withdrawal can be more difficult than heroin withdrawal. The majority of smokers have unsuccessfully tried to quit smoking at least once. Because of the health benefits associated with quitting smoking, such as reducing the risk of cancer and heart disease, experts offer numerous opinions on how to quit smoking and how to prevent young people from starting.

Many health professionals maintain that nicotine replacement therapy (NRT) can reduce the negative symptoms associated with nicotine withdrawal, such as irritability, inability to concentrate, and hunger, and thereby make quitting easier. NRTs are available in such forms as a patch, gum, lozenges, and inhalers that administer controlled doses of nicotine to the smoker and help quell cravings for a cigarette. Experts contend that combining NRT with emotional support can significantly increase the success rate of smokers trying to quit. As stated by physician Donald J. Brideau: "Although the benefits of cessation are clear, people often fail in their attempts to stop smoking because of the addictive properties of nicotine. However, a strong smoking cessation program that incorporates behavioral therapy and nicotine replacement products can increase the likelihood of success."

Others argue that the best way to reduce smoking is to prevent young people from ever lighting up, as most smokers try their first cigarette when they are teenagers. According to the American Heart Association, more than 90 percent of smokers started smoking before they were eighteen, and every day three thousand children try their first cigarette. Public health officials propose various methods for reducing teen smoking. According to journalist David Gergen, "Health experts and economists generally agree that short of banning tobacco altogether—which adult Americans are not prepared to do—we can make sizable cutbacks in teen smoking by adopting a three-pronged strategy: Increase prices, restrict advertising, and make vendors enforce age limits more rigorously." Gergen and others contend that the focus of the war on tobacco should be on children and preventing addiction to nicotine.

The question of how smoking can be reduced is discussed by the authors in the following chapter.

Government Programs Can Reduce Smoking

by the National Cancer Policy Board, Institute of Medicine, and National Research Council

About the authors: *The National Cancer Policy Board, Institute of Medicine, and National Research Council are affiliated with the National Academy of Sciences, a private, nonprofit academy of scholars dedicated to the advancement of science and technology.*

Growing attention is focused on how states can prevent deaths due to tobacco use. Thus state governors, state legislators, and their staffs must decide whether to fund tobacco control programs, and, if they do, how much to spend on them.

The National Cancer Policy Board (a joint program of the Institute of Medicine and the National Research Council) is charged with carrying out policy analyses to help the nation deal with cancer; in 1997, it quickly identified tobacco's role as the foremost cause of cancer deaths as its first topic of concern. The board followed debates taking place in state capitals throughout 1998 and 1999, and decided in July 1999, in consultation with the Board on Health Promotion and Disease Prevention of the Institute of Medicine, that it would be useful to summarize evidence about the effectiveness of state tobacco control programs and to briefly describe those programs for state government officials.

Tobacco control will likely remain on the agenda of many states for several years. Public health advocates, tobacco firms, tobacco growers, retailers, and the general public have all been drawn into the debate. This report does not address the merit of tobacco control compared to alternative uses of state funds or attempt to balance the interests of contending stakeholders; instead, it focuses on the narrower question of whether state tobacco control programs can reduce smoking and save lives. As states contemplate increasing their tobacco control efforts, many have asked if such programs can make a difference. The evidence is clear: They can.

From "State Programs Can Reduce Tobacco Use," by the National Cancer Policy Board, Institute of Medicine, and National Research Council, www.nap.edu, 2000. Copyright © 2000 National Academy of Sciences. Reprinted with permission of the National Academy Press.

The Stakes Are High

Tobacco use kills more Americans each year than any other cause. The estimated 430,000 deaths attributed to tobacco use annually are far more than those caused by illegal drugs, homicides, suicides, AIDS, motor vehicle accidents, and alcohol combined. Lung cancer kills more Americans than breast and prostate cancer combined, and tobacco accounts for over 30% of all cancer deaths and a comparable fraction of deaths due to heart and lung diseases. Yet despite these risks, many, many people start smoking each year. In 1996, over 1.8 million people became daily smokers, two-thirds of them (1.2 million) under age 18.

Over the past decade, states have moved to the forefront of tobacco control. Starting with California in 1988, and followed by Massachusetts, Arizona, Oregon, and other states, referenda have increased tobacco excise taxes and dedicated a fraction of the revenues to reducing tobacco use. Legislatures in other states—such as Alaska, Hawaii, Maryland, Michigan, New Jersey, New York, and Washington—have increased tobacco taxes substantially, raising questions about how much of the revenue should go to tobacco control. In addition, settlements of lawsuits against tobacco firms to recoup state monies spent through Medicaid have now resulted in individual state revenue streams (in Florida, Minnesota, Mississippi, and Texas) or in revenues anticipated through the Master Settlement Agreement with the other states and territories signed in 1998. In aggregate, these agreements could transfer as much as $246 billion from tobacco firms to states over the next 25 years.

What Is the Evidence?

The best evidence for the effectiveness of state tobacco control programs comes from comparing states with different intensities of tobacco control, as measured by funding levels and "aggressiveness." For example, when California and Massachusetts mounted programs that were more "intense" than those of other states, they showed greater decreases in tobacco use compared to states that were part of the American Stop Smoking Intervention Study (ASSIST) funded by the National Cancer Institute. From 1989 to 1993, when the Massachusetts program began, California had the largest and most aggressive tobacco control program in the nation, and it showed a singular decline in cigarette consumption that was over 50% faster than the national average.

> *"Tobacco [is one of the] foremost cause[s] of cancer deaths."*

A recent evaluation of the Massachusetts tobacco control program showed a 15% decline in adult smoking—compared to very little change nationally— thus reducing the number of smokers there by 153,000 between 1993 and 1999. States that were part of the ASSIST program, in turn, devoted more resources to tobacco control than did other states except Massachusetts and California, and they showed in aggregate a 7% reduction in tobacco consumption per capita from 1993 to 1996 compared to non-ASSIST states. Such a "dose-response" effect is strong evidence that state programs have an impact, that more tobacco control correlates with less tobacco use, and that the reduction coincides with the intensification of tobacco control efforts.

A second line of evidence comes from observing effects on tobacco consumption beyond those associated with price. When tobacco prices rise, sales should drop, and when prices drop, sales should rise. Yet price alone does not explain the observed consumption patterns. In the first 2 years after Oregon's ballot initiative was implemented, for example, cigarette consumption dropped by over 11%, which is 5% more than would be expected from the price increase alone. The reported decreases in tobacco use in Alaska, California, and Florida similarly exceed what would be expected from price increases alone. Moreover, when cigarette prices dropped nationwide during 1992–1994, consumption rose in states with small tobacco control efforts but did not rise in 11 of 14 ASSIST states; consumption also plateaued in California and Massachusetts. This suggests that tobacco control measures limited the increase in tobacco sales expected as a result of a price drop.

> "The best evidence for the effectiveness of state tobacco control programs comes from comparing states with different intensities of tobacco control."

In the review of tobacco control program elements that follows, results are reported in ranges, and sometimes those ranges are large. It is generally quite difficult to attribute a reduction in tobacco use to any single factor; often, many factors work in parallel. The underlying message is quite clear, however: Multifaceted state tobacco control programs are effective in reducing tobacco use.

Counteradvertising and Education

Counteradvertising and public education campaigns have become standard elements of tobacco control, although their funding levels and aggressiveness vary considerably among the states. Counteradvertising campaigns can convey a variety of messages and can be aimed at different audiences. An evaluation of the California tobacco control program concluded that it was most effective in its early years, when the highest-impact advertisements emphasized deceptive practices undertaken by tobacco firms. Evaluators concluded that the program became less effective when spending for counteradvertising dropped (from $16 million in 1991 to $6.6 million by 1995), and when the advertisements began to focus on health risks rather than tobacco industry practices. As a result, the program's advisory committee made its foremost 1997 goal to "vigorously expose tobacco industry tactics." A "natural experiment" underway in Florida may provide further insight. The Florida Pilot Program, funded by that state's tobacco settlement, created the edgy "Truth Campaign" and SWAT (Students Working

Against Tobacco) program. During its first year, tobacco use among youths decreased dramatically. The second-year budgets for both programs were seriously threatened in the Florida legislature—at one point facing extinction—but funding was partially restored. The program director was removed and the counteradvertising campaign was said to be heading "in a new direction." The budget for public media is slated to drop from $24 million to $18 million in the second year. If the rate of decline in tobacco consump-

> *"School-based tobacco prevention programs . . . are most effective when the message is delivered repeatedly and is taken . . . seriously."*

tion among youths stalls in Florida, as it did in California after 1994, this would provide further evidence that the "dose" of tobacco control predicts its impact.

School-based tobacco prevention programs are also part of state tobacco control programs. The effectiveness of school-based programs varies. They are most effective when the message is delivered repeatedly and is taken as seriously and promoted as powerfully as are other forms of drug abuse education. Properly implemented school programs can, however, lower smoking prevalence from 25% to 60%. These programs have been evaluated repeatedly, and in 1994 the Centers for Disease Control and Prevention (CDC) produced a set of guidelines for school-based programs. States will want to take care in implementing school-based programs, however, because they can consume considerable resources to little effect; a 1996 meta-analysis showed only a modest impact for most programs. The 1994 Institute of Medicine report *Growing Up Tobacco Free* noted the variable results of school-based programs but concluded that they should be part of a comprehensive tobacco control strategy because educating school-age children and adolescents about the consequences of tobacco use is clearly important to sustain a smoke-free norm.

Experimentation with the content and style of counteradvertising and education programs will and should continue, subject to evaluation to enable improvements and increase their impact. With that in mind, the American Legacy Foundation was established with funding from the 1998 Master Settlement Agreement. Its duties will include funding and oversight of a national counteradvertising campaign. Many states are also planning major increases in their counteradvertising and education initiatives.

Establishing Smoke-Free Workplaces and Public Spaces

The main impetus for smoke-free environments grew from concern about exposing nonsmokers to the toxic effects of tobacco smoke. Making worksites, schools, and homes smoke-free zones is a powerful strategy for reducing tobacco use overall because it boosts quit rates and reduces consumption. A 1996 review, for example, estimated that smoke-free workplaces reduced the number of smokers by 5% on average (meaning that almost one in five smokers quit, as smoking prevalence is about 25%) and reduced use among continuing smokers by 10%. Another review attributed over 22% of the tobacco consumption drop in Australia between 1988 and 1995, and almost 13% of the drop in the United States between 1988 and 1994, to smoke-free workplace policies. The death toll and ill-health attributable to involuntary smoking are thoroughly documented in a Surgeon General's report, a report from the federal Environmental Protection Agency (EPA), and a study by the California EPA. Federal regulations prohibit smoking in federal buildings and in airplanes. In some states and localities, laws and ordinances proscribe smoking in workplaces, schools, public spaces, restaurants, and other sites. Creating smoke-free workplaces and public spaces reduces tobacco use among smokers while reducing involuntary smoking by nonsmokers. Smoking restrictions have been a major focus of some states' tobacco control efforts and are a central thrust of much activity at the county and city levels.

Increasing Prices Through Taxation

Raising the price of tobacco products through taxation is one of the fastest and most effective ways to discourage children and youths from starting to smoke and to encourage smokers to quit. In 1994 and 1998, the Institute of Medicine recommended price increases of $2 per pack (or equivalent for other tobacco products), based on levels needed to approach the health goals in *Healthy People 2000* and to approach parity with other countries that have effective tobacco control programs. Wholesale prices have increased an average of $0.65 per pack nationwide since the Master Settlement Agreement was signed in 1998, the federal excise tax was raised to $0.24 per pack in the Balanced Budget Act of 1997, and six states now have excise taxes over $0.75 per pack. Even high-tax states remain short of the Institute's recommended level, however, and 20 states have excise taxes below $0.20 per pack. The wholesale price and excise tax increases do not necessarily imply equal increases in retail prices that consumers see, as discounts to retailers are commonplace for tobacco products, and local business factors are important. It is nonetheless clear that the floor for prices have risen, even if the ceiling is variable.

> *"Making worksites, schools, and homes smoke-free zones is a powerful strategy for reducing tobacco use overall because it boosts quit rates and reduces consumption."*

Economists have reached a consensus that a cigarette price increase of 10% will decrease total consumption by about 4%. Most economists now believe the response is larger (i.e., about 8%) among youths, based on recent studies. Conclusions about whether price disproportionately affects children and youths are based on fewer data than larger studies of total tobacco consumption. A classic 1990 study showed that responsiveness to price (elasticity of demand) increased over time from 1970 to 1985 but found little difference between adults and youths. A more recent review of more elaborate studies showed elasticities in the range noted above; it also found that youths were more sensitive to price, as demonstrated by fewer youths starting to smoke and reduced consumption among continuing youth smokers. An April 1998 report from the Congressional Budget Office reviewed many studies of price and consumption. It found unequivocal evidence that increased prices reduce use, although details about the mechanisms and effects are not completely understood.

Proposals to increase cigarette taxes face strong opposition. (Interestingly, tobacco taxes are one of the few taxes for which a majority of Americans favor increases, especially if the revenues derived are dedicated to tobacco control.) The principal policy concern is that tobacco taxes are regressive, because tobacco use is more common among people with low incomes, and thus the poor spend proportionately more of their incomes on cigarettes. Tax increases are actually less regressive than simple projections suggest, however, because the poor are more sensitive to price and their consumption falls more sharply when prices rise. The World Bank supports increasing tobacco excise taxes for its public health impact and notes that judgments about regressiveness "should be over the distributional impact of the entire tax and expenditure system, and less on particular taxes in isolation."

Governors and legislators have raised concerns about increasing prices on tobacco because revenues from excise taxes might drop, along with payments expected under the Master Settlement Agreement (because payments to states are tied to sales). States concerned about revenue loss have an effective option—raising the state excise tax rate. The World Bank notes that "empirical evidence shows that raised tobacco taxes bring greater [overall] tobacco tax revenues." Reduced consumption will also ultimately lead to lower health costs to states through Medicaid and other health programs. In one study, the health benefits due to lower rates of heart attack and stroke began quickly, and the health benefits more than offset the program's costs after 1 year. The immediate economic and health benefits are later compounded by reductions in cancer and other chronic diseases.

Supporting Treatment Programs for Tobacco Dependence

Nicotine addiction, like other addictions, is a treatable condition. Treatment programs for tobacco dependence can work. States have two major roles in treating tobacco dependence: (1) educating tobacco-dependent people about their treatment options through public health programs, and (2) ensuring that medical programs cover and reimburse the costs of the treatments. As of 1997, only 22 states and the District of Columbia covered such treatment under Medicaid, leading to a recommendation by D.C. Barker, C.T. Orleans, and H.H. Schauffler that state Medicaid agencies "incorporate explicit language into their managed-care contracts, policy briefs, lawsuit provisions, and Medicaid formularies." States can take guidance on policies to improve tobacco treatments from a report by the Center for the Advancement of Health.

Community-based resources such as centralized "quitlines" and workplace wellness programs can increase access to cessation programs. State governments are among the largest employers in most states, and a major employer in all. States can ensure that their employees have access to treatment through their health plans, and smoking bans in state buildings can increase cessation and reduce tobacco use among continuing smokers. States can also pass laws to create smoke-free businesses, public buildings, and worksites. State and local media campaigns that reinforce nonsmoking norms also enhance motivation to quit, reduce tobacco use among those who continue to smoke, and prevent relapse.

> *"Treatment programs for tobacco dependence can work."*

Much can be done to improve access to and the effectiveness of treatment programs within medical systems. More than 70% of smokers visit a primary health care provider at least once a year. Systematic reviews conclude that routine, repeated advice and support can increase smoking cessation rates by 2- to 3-fold. Physicians, nurses, psychologists, dentists, and other health professionals are more likely to give such advice and support if they practice in a system that encourages such behavior through practice-based systems for tracking smoking status, office-based written materials for smokers to take home, training of health professionals in screening and advising patients, coverage of cessation programs by health plans, and reimbursement for treatments by payers (including Medicaid).

Most people who use tobacco—at all ages—express a desire to quit, but only a small fraction succeed on their own. Although many who do quit do so without formal treatment, treatment clearly improves cessation rates. Controlled studies generally report 30%–35% cessation rates at 1 year for intensive treatments and 10%–20% cessation rates for less-intensive treatments. Treatment for addiction to tobacco products ranks high in cost-effectiveness among health program spending options. Programs that combine behavioral therapies with pharmacotherapies (i.e., medications) have the best results, and evidence-based guidelines recommend that all smokers should be offered both. Behavioral programs can be delivered in group settings (in person) or individually (in person or by telephone). Food and Drug Administration (FDA)-approved medications include nicotine replacement agents (in gum, patch, nasal spray, or inhaler delivery systems) and the antidepressant drug bupropion.

Treatment works, but there is ample room for improvement. Despite evidence of its effectiveness, relatively few smokers seek out formal treatment, and relapse rates are high. Improving smoking cessation success rates would be especially important in certain target populations. For example, Massachusetts placed an emphasis on reducing smoking among pregnant women because it would produce long-lasting benefits for the prospective mothers and reduce risks to their children. As a result, the number of mothers who smoked during pregnancy dropped by almost 48% during 1990–1996, a rate far ahead that of any other state.

It has long been illegal—in every state—to sell tobacco products to minors, but until recently, enforcement was lax. The federal Synar Amendment ties federal block grant monies to improved compliance with state laws proscribing such sales. States risk reduced payments from the Substance Abuse and Mental Health Administration if they fail to meet compliance targets. The federal government has never withheld state funds based on the Synar Amendment, but such withholding is under discussion for several states that have not met Synar targets. Enforcement of youth sales, with mandatory ID-card inspection of those 26 and younger, was the central thrust of a 1996 FDA tobacco regulation. This part of the regulation remains in force pending a U.S. Supreme Court ruling about FDA's jurisdiction over tobacco products. States now have FDA contracts to enforce and monitor youth sales. Several reports have noted that enforcing laws against sales to minors can reduce tobacco consumption. Although one 1997 study of enforcement showed no decline in youth smoking, the authors attributed the lack of impact to insufficient merchant compliance and developed a model approach that is being used in Massachusetts. Excessive focus or exclusive reliance on youth access restrictions can siphon resources and political will from more powerful tobacco control measures. Yet all U.S. jurisdictions have youth access laws, and if those laws are to become meaningful, they must be enforced.

Monitoring Performance and Evaluating Programs

Today's tobacco control programs build on decades of research and demonstrations. The scale and scope of tobacco control in the United States—particularly in the most aggressive states—has grown considerably over the past decade, and the proper balance and content of program elements are the subjects of continuing debate. Tobacco control can improve over time only if (a) its elements are assessed, (b) state programs that choose different strategies are compared, and (c) research to improve the programs is carried out. Governors and state legislators, moreover, need to be able to be accountable for the use of public dollars. This does not imply that results will be quick; significant reductions in tobacco use take years even in states where tobacco control has clearly been effective.

Performance monitoring of public health programs is receiving increased attention. Measures to monitor the performance of tobacco control programs are in place, and efforts are underway to improve them. Without specified goals and ways of measuring progress, the effectiveness of public monies spent on such programs is hard to judge, so state tobacco control programs should include resources for evaluation and research as part of a comprehensive tobacco control program.

Government Regulation Will Not Reduce Smoking

by John E. Calfee

About the author: *John E. Calfee is a resident scholar at the American Enterprise Institute, a conservative public policy research organization, and the author of* Fear of Persuasion: A New Perspective on Advertising and Regulation.

The war on tobacco has turned upside down. For decades, as new information emerged about the health effects of smoking, public policy relentlessly emphasized individual decision-making. This brought real achievements—notably, a 40 percent reduction in U.S. per capita cigarette consumption between 1975 and 1993.

Some half dozen years ago, however, the battle over tobacco entered a new phase. The focus shifted from smoking to the tobacco industry. A new view took hold. In this view, smoking is caused primarily by deceptive advertising targeted at young people, the manipulation of nicotine to maintain addiction, and the suppression of information on the harm caused by smoking. Smokers should be seen as victims of these forces. And the solution is drastic reform of the industry itself.

The Tobacco Settlement

This new vision rapidly coalesced into policy. Several states raised tobacco taxes in order to protect smokers from their own preferences and to fund anti-smoking campaigns and research. Federal action followed, notably the attempt of the Food and Drug Administration (FDA) to regulate cigarettes as nicotine-delivery devices. At the same time came an astonishing barrage of litigation, generating multi-billion-dollar settlements in Mississippi, Texas, Florida, and . . . Minnesota. A June 1997 agreement [commonly called the tobacco settlement] among plaintiff attorneys, state attorneys general, and the tobacco industry provided a model for comprehensive federal legislative proposals, over which debate continues to this day.

All of this activity tends to focus on a concrete goal and a specific set of tools. The goal is to reduce teen smoking rapidly by half or more, with a corresponding reduction in adult smoking as the teens get older. The tools: elimination of advertising seen by teens, price increases of up to $2 per pack, antismoking campaigns, litigation to penalize the industry financially, "look-back" penalties on the industry if teen smoking does not decrease, and FDA jurisdiction over the development of safer cigarettes.

The new approach will almost certainly fail. In fact, disturbing symptoms of failure have already begun to appear. Teen smoking has increased substantially from 1991 to 1998. That has caught people's attention, but probably more alarming is a little-noticed change in the trend of overall consumption. After 15 years of sharp annual declines, per-capita cigarette consumption has hardly dropped since 1993.

The Settlement Will Not Reduce Teen Smoking

Quite aside from these numbers, there are compelling reasons to believe that the central elements of the plan cannot do what they are supposed to do. Consider prices, the single most important tool in the new thinking. Current proposals would raise federal taxes by a dollar or two—former surgeon general C. Everett Koop and former FDA commissioner David Kessler have proposed $1.50. This is expected to cut teenage smoking by a third or more. The logic is that teens don't realize they will get hooked on nicotine if they smoke, but they will react strongly to higher prices. This seems most unlikely. With teen smokers consuming an average of eight cigarettes a day, there is little reason to expect an extra five or ten cents per cigarette to stop them from smoking. And in fact, the biggest drop in teenage smoking—a nearly one-third decline in the late 1970s—occurred when cigarette prices were also going down (by about 15 percent). On the other hand, prices have been stable or slightly rising since 1991, even as teen smoking increased. In the United Kingdom, where cigarettes already cost twice as much as in the United States, teenagers smoke at about the same rate as they do here.

What about advertising? Tell a teenager that advertising is the reason he smokes, and you will probably convince a teenager that you are out of touch with reality. Repeated statistical analyses have failed to detect a substantial effect on consumption from advertising. One may quibble

> *"Teen smoking has increased substantially from 1991 to 1998."*

about the details of individual studies, but the overall results are unmistakable. If advertising's effect on cigarette consumption were substantial, it would have been detected by now.

FDA regulation, if it comes to pass, will be institutionalized frustration. The new rules on advertising cannot reduce teen smoking, because advertising restrictions can hardly prevent what advertising never caused. Safer cigarettes (with less tar and nicotine) will be stymied, as the FDA vigorously implements policies reflecting the public-health community's hostility to safer smoking and new types of cigarettes. [FDA regulation failed to become law.]

There remain the anti-smoking campaigns. Often tried, they have generally had disappointing results. The people who design these campaigns tend to act on their own pet theories (they think teens are being duped by advertising) and to pursue political goals. Anti-smoking advertising, like the anti-smoking movement generally, has therefore become a vehicle for the new view that the proper target is the tobacco industry rather than smoking.

> *"Tell a teenager that advertising is the reason he smokes, and you will probably convince a teenager that you are out of touch with reality."*

Thus in California, Massachusetts, and Florida, government-funded campaigns tell kids they can't trust tobacco companies. This non-news is unlikely to cause kids to toss their cigarettes away, but it is consistent with political objectives such as new anti-smoking measures. Two anti-smoking scholars recently praised California's anti-smoking ads for challenging "the dominant view that public health problems reflect personal habits," and they noted that "it is political action and attitudes, rather than personal behavior, on which counter-ads are focused." In fact, the most effective anti-smoking ads probably come from the pharmaceutical firms that market smoking-cessation products. These firms have a financial incentive to communicate the information and strategies that will make people get serious about quitting smoking.

Prisoners of Preconceptions

Why do so many well-meaning people pursue measures that cannot achieve their goals? The short answer is that they are prisoners of their own preconceptions. They reject the idea that well-informed people ever choose to smoke; they believe advertising has a power that it has never had; they are ignorant of the history of cigarette marketing; and they give unquestioning credence to economic studies of the "price elasticity" of cigarettes that are of dubious value for the purposes to which they are put.

For the fact is that there is a deep conflict between what anti-smoking campaigners want to be true and what is true. This has fostered a strategy of deception and distortion. Such a strategy can succeed in the short run because of the peculiar circumstances of the tobacco market. Anti-smoking activists learned years ago that when they stretched the facts, those who corrected them were dismissed as industry hacks. This led to the amazing discovery that those who oppose smoking can wander far beyond the boundaries of good science (even in esteemed outlets such as the *Journal of the American Medical Association,* or

JAMA) and still see their words accepted and amplified by an unquestioning media. Naturally, anti-smoking campaigners have seized this opportunity, introducing numerous absurdities into the everyday thinking of scholars, regulatory officials, journalists, and politicians. Thus we have been told that cigarettes are the most advertised product in America (wrong by more than an order of magnitude), that research has finally nailed down the connection between marketing and smoking by kids, and that secret industry documents show that the problem all along has been the targeting of youth. Such misinformation is routinely accepted and repeated as if it were the truth.

Here is a concrete example. One of the most often cited *JAMA* studies—in fact, the *only* non-governmental study the FDA cited in its regulatory initiative that actually used market data rather than surveys and the like—claimed to demonstrate that advertising for the first women's brands, in the late 1970s, caused a surge in smoking by teenage girls. The authors used sales data (not advertising data), took their figures from an unpublished student paper, dropped the three of six brands that did not fit their thesis, mistook billions of cigarettes sold for billions of *dollars'* worth of cigarettes sold (a forty-fold error), and concluded to much acclaim that massive advertising had fundamentally altered the market. This utterly useless study is repeatedly cited as proof that advertising causes teen smoking. This kind of thing would not happen in an ordinary intellectual environment.

Sometimes, history has been rewritten. Despite what the FDA says, the discovery that people smoke to get nicotine is not new, and neither is the fact that manufacturers strongly influence the amount of nicotine in cigarette smoke. In the late 1960s and early 1970s, maintaining adequate nicotine levels in low-tar cigarettes was widely believed to be the key to progress against the diseases caused by smoking. This belief—which originated with public-health scholars, not the tobacco industry—was so pervasive that *Consumer Reports* declared in 1972 that "efforts should be made to popularize ways of delivering frequent doses of nicotine to addicts without filling their lungs with smoke."

The National Cancer Institute and the Department of Agriculture maintained a large program devoted to developing improved strains of tobacco (containing more nicotine). A biotech firm hired by a tobacco company to cultivate one of those variants in South America (to avoid growing it in the United States) was recently accused of criminal behavior for doing so in violation of a law that was repealed in 1991. Amazingly, the FDA regarded this episode as a prime justification for regulating the tobacco industry. Again, this kind of thing would not happen in an ordinary intellectual environment.

Costs of Attacking the Tobacco Industry

Clearly, the new strategy of attacking the tobacco industry rather than smoking is producing little if any benefit. The costs, on the other hand, are large and growing.

First, there are costs to public health. We are abandoning the only approach to smoking-reduction that is likely to succeed: reliance on individual responsibility. This point was eloquently stated by a George Washington University physician, Larry H. Pastor, in a letter to the editor of the *Journal of the American Medical Association* in 1996. Describing the dubious proposition that tobacco litigation will make people quit smoking, Pastor noted that exactly the opposite could easily happen,

> because some smokers will feel reinforced in externalizing blame onto "the tobacco industry" and thereby fail to take the difficult steps necessary to confront their smoking addiction. The more such personal injury litigation succeeds, the more some will comfort themselves with the rationalization that, if they develop tobacco-related illness, they can sue the cigarette makers and obtain a lucrative reward.

The strategy of blaming the industry for smoking is getting in the way of efforts to discourage smoking itself.

Second, there is the matter of who will pay the higher cigarette taxes. A hallmark of the U.S. market is that most smoking is done by people of modest means. And the idea that smokers impose financial costs on others has little foundation. To say that blue-collar smokers should pay more for their habit because they cannot protect themselves from manipulation by the tobacco companies—and then watch them continue to smoke while the nation collects billions of dollars from their pockets to spend on other citizens—

> *"The strategy of blaming the industry for smoking is getting in the way of efforts to discourage smoking itself."*

is a sorry combination of paternalism and hypocrisy. Perhaps these smokers should simply be allowed to pursue their freely chosen course without financial penalty. At any rate, with teens buying only about 2 percent of the cigarettes sold, we know that a massive tax increase designed to stop teen smoking will be paid almost entirely by non-teens, most of them poor or lower-middle class.

The third cost of the new approach lies in the danger of creating a government stake in continued smoking. The Clinton administration wanted to raise cigarette taxes so it could transfer tens of billions of dollars from smokers to its favorite domestic-policy initiatives. Far more dangerous than a mere tax-grab, this plan would have worked only if most smokers continued to smoke and pay the higher taxes. . . . The history of the anti-smoking movement makes clear that the toughest places in which to make progress are countries like Japan, Thailand, and China—that is, nations with a large state investment in smoking.

Fourth, as the new approach is applied to products other than tobacco, it will be hugely disruptive—and it cannot easily be confined to tobacco. This is so for three reasons. (1) The underlying principle, that marketers are responsible for the behavior of anyone who buys their products, is indiscriminate. It is not intrinsically more relevant to tobacco than to, say, automobiles, alcohol, or red meat. (2) The tools of the new regime are too tempting. They operate by combining political opportunism with the legal means for extracting financial payments. Once launched, the process is self-perpetuating. The plaintiff attorneys who are engineering today's mass tobacco litigation honed their skills in asbestos litigation, and they are eager to move on to other arenas. (3) These methods and tools are not easily dismantled. They are greatly prized by the litigation community, advocacy groups, politicians who like to spend taxes, even academics in search of funding. Wresting such valuable tools away from those who have become accustomed to using them could be very difficult.

> *"The only effective way of combating the harmful effects of smoking in the long run is to encourage an enduring sense of personal responsibility."*

Finally, the new approach to tobacco carries the cost of degrading the intellectual environment. This is no trivial matter. The public-health community's power depends on information, credibility, and the consequent ability to persuade. That power can be dissipated if it is carelessly misused (as it has been), and once lost, it cannot easily be regained. As journalist Carl Cannon noted, after describing some grossly untrue statements from the White House during the debate over tobacco legislation in the Senate in 1998, "The problem is that in employing the devilishly effective—but not always truthful—language of political campaigns, the good guys risk losing the moral high ground." Deception is not—at least should not be, in a free society—a viable long-run strategy.

The time has come, then, for public policy toward tobacco to return to its roots. The only effective way of combating the harmful effects of smoking in the long run is to encourage an enduring sense of personal responsibility— among smokers, their families, and physicians. But that's not all. Two decades of an absurd hostility to safer smoking and safer tobacco must end. We have forgotten that in the 1950s, the pronouncements of cancer researchers created a demand for cigarettes with less tar and nicotine, and the cigarette manufacturers responded with a speed that in hindsight seems miraculous. Today, instead of talking about draconian taxes and sweeping infringements on commercial speech, we should let the competitive market again serve smokers—just as it does everyone else.

International Cooperation Is Needed to Reduce Smoking

by David Satcher

About the author: *David Satcher has been the surgeon general of the United States since 1998.*

Tobacco use is pandemic. If the countries of the world do not act to reduce tobacco use, in the next 20 to 30 years 10 million people per year will be dying from the effects of this addictive drug. Individual countries acting in isolation cannot combat the problem. As Director General Gro Harlem Brundtland of the World Health Organization has noted, "the globalization of the tobacco industry's marketing strategies has contributed to a breakdown in local and national cultural barriers to tobacco use." Tobacco use is truly a global health problem, requiring countries to cooperate in strong international action even as they tailor their tobacco control efforts to their own unique circumstances.

In October 2000, representatives from 150 countries convened in Geneva, Switzerland, to begin negotiating the first international agreement on tobacco control in the 50-year history of the World Health Organization. Due to be completed by 2003, this agreement is known as the Framework Convention on Tobacco Control (FCTC). The FCTC is expected to provide a means to stop the growth of tobacco use through a combination of national and international actions.

A Growing Global Health Problem

The percentage of deaths worldwide that is attributable to tobacco use is projected to double from 6% in 1990 to 12.3% in 2020, surpassing diarrheal diseases, perinatal diseases, and tuberculosis. Globally, about 4 million deaths per year are attributable to smoking. Over the next 30 years, if nothing is done to stop current trends, the tobacco-related death toll could rise to 10 million per year. Most—7 million—of these preventable deaths will occur in the develop-

From "With Four Million Deaths Per Year Attributable to Smoking: Why We Need an International Agreement on Tobacco Control," by David Satcher, *American Journal of Public Health*, February 2001.

ing world. Over the past 20 years, there has been a gradual decrease in cigarette consumption in the developed countries and an increase in the developing countries. "Very rarely do we have the ability to predict an epidemic so far in the future and also have the knowledge to prevent it" is the blunt analysis from the 11th World Conference on Tobacco or Health.

The world has responded to communicable diseases with efforts such as the World Health Organization's Roll Back Malaria Initiative and UNAIDS [United Nations Program on HIV/AIDS]; similar international action is needed to counter the looming expansion of preventable tobacco-related diseases and death. The cross-border elements of the tobacco problem can best be addressed through coordinated international efforts involving not just traditional health ministries but also ministries of commerce, justice, and foreign affairs. The areas of tobacco control most needing coordinated international activity are antismuggling measures, advertising and sponsorship restrictions, ingredient testing methods, package design and labeling guidelines, price harmonization, treatment of tobacco dependence, and information sharing. Progress in tobacco control can be made as countries coordinate their efforts, at least at a regional level.

Cigarette smuggling is an important element of the international tobacco problem. About one fifth of annual worldwide cigarette production is exported. Only two thirds of exported cigarettes show up as legal imports in other countries each year. The "missing" cigarettes, about 6% of all those manufactured, are most likely smuggled around the world. The European Commission

> *"Individual countries acting in isolation cannot combat the [tobacco] problem."*

has argued, on the basis of its analyses of tobacco industry documents in a recently filed lawsuit, that tobacco companies are heavily involved in smuggling schemes.

Cigarette smuggling provides consumers with cigarettes at below-market prices, making cigarette smuggling a public health problem as well as a law enforcement problem. These cheaper cigarettes thwart national health policies that use price increases to reduce tobacco consumption. Tobacco companies argue against raising tobacco taxes because they say higher prices encourage smuggling from low-tax to high-tax countries; however, some analysts have found that poor enforcement of border controls is a better predictor of the level of smuggling than price differentials between countries. In any case, the lower price of smuggled cigarettes leads to greater consumption than would occur otherwise.

Advertising Spreads the Use of Tobacco

As the large transnational tobacco companies such as Philip Morris and British American Tobacco (BAT) move into new markets around the world, they spend enormous amounts on advertising and promotion. The tobacco companies know, and public health research clearly demonstrates, that "tobacco advertising increases tobacco consumption," [as stated by H. Saffer and F. Chaloupka]. Young people are especially affected by advertising messages, even when the messages are not specifically addressed to them.

Foreign cigarette advertising makes a deep impression in overseas markets. In China, highly advertised brands achieve wide recognition and consumer preference. The prevalence of smoking among Chinese adult men is 63%, among male middle

> *"Cigarette smuggling provides consumers with cigarettes at below-market prices, making cigarette smuggling a public health problem as well as a law enforcement problem."*

school students 23%. However, the potential effect of new advertising campaigns could be most dramatic for Chinese women, of whom only 3.8% now smoke, and girls, of whom only 5% now smoke.

Tobacco companies adapt their advertising practices for developing countries, often across borders. Although advertisements for cigarettes are banned in the mass media in Malaysia, the international tobacco companies use sham businesses to circumvent the ban. Travel agencies, record shops, bistros, and clothing stores, in a process known as brand stretching, carry tobacco brand names such as Peter Stuyvesant Travel or Salem Cool Planet. The companies sponsor contests for young men and women, and television documentaries show the winners enjoying their prizes. These documentaries are permeated with advertisements for non-tobacco-related businesses that just happen to have the same names as tobacco brands. Not coincidentally, these television programs are received in neighboring Thailand and Singapore, which ban all forms of tobacco advertising and sponsorship.

The FCTC should be able to ensure cooperation among nations to address these transnational issues. By agreeing to general provisions in the FCTC itself and to more detailed provisions in related protocols, nations should be able to coordinate their efforts to combat smuggling and restrict advertising more effectively than they could through individual or bilateral efforts.

Surveillance Sheds Light on the Problem

Data and data analysis are crucial tools in communicating the nature and scope of the tobacco problem to policymakers and the public and in monitoring progress in reducing tobacco use. Data are needed on the prevalence of tobacco use, trends in tobacco consumption, the disease burden from tobacco use, tobacco control laws and regulations, and programmatic interventions, as well as on tobacco production, marketing, and trade.

Many countries do not have these data. At the 11th World Conference on Tobacco or Health in August 2000, where I released the report *Reducing Tobacco Use*, the American Cancer Society, together with the US Centers for Disease

Control and Prevention and the World Health Organization, released a reference book titled *Tobacco Country Profiles*, which provides the most current and comprehensive documentation of the status of the tobacco use epidemic in 197 countries and territories. After an exhaustive search, its authors were able to provide data on adult smoking prevalence in 158 of the 197 countries and territories and on youth smoking prevalence in 150, but most of the national estimates were from subnational surveys. The authors were able to provide estimates of smoking-attributable deaths in only 44 developed countries.

Clearly, much work needs to be done across borders to assist countries in developing and implementing systems for monitoring the many aspects of the tobacco use problem. Many countries will also need assistance in using these data for their own policy actions and comprehensive tobacco control programs.

US Efforts Are Crucial

The United States is committed to supporting the FCTC and playing a leadership role in its development. This country has an impressive resume in the tobacco control field: few countries have invested more in research, surveillance, and evaluation. The United States has pioneered work on regulatory approaches to tobacco control, tough restrictions on secondhand smoke in federal buildings, comprehensive enforcement of minimum-age-of-sale laws, development and promotion of effective smoking cessation therapies, and litigation to make tobacco

> *"Much work needs to be done across borders to assist countries in developing and implementing systems for monitoring the many aspects of the tobacco use problem."*

companies accountable for their actions, and it has enacted restrictions that prevent US Foreign Service personnel from promoting the sale of US tobacco products overseas.

Other countries are also established leaders in tobacco control and have much to contribute to the global fight against tobacco. Canada leads the world in warning labels, with its new and graphic system of labels for all tobacco product packages, which became effective in January 2001; Canada also implemented tax increases to reduce consumption in the 1980s. Finland achieved large reductions in cigarette use among men, beginning in the 1970s, with its vigorous national programs against heart disease. Norway instituted one of the first complete advertising bans. Thailand has reduced smoking prevalence among males, in large part through a national advertising ban and a cigarette tax increase. It plans to add Canadian-style package warning labels soon. In the United Kingdom, tax increases have been effective in reducing consumption. Australia has extensive restrictions on tobacco advertising and sports sponsorship, as well as strong warning labels on packages and a highly regarded media campaign.

The most powerful export of the United States is its popular culture. The tobacco industry has taken advantage of this reality and, through its advertising, represented smoking as a central element of American culture. In the Philippines, images of Americans dominate tobacco advertising on television. The Marlboro Man has replaced Uncle Sam as an American icon. Tragically, in many developing countries, young people and women, hungering for American culture, turn to American cigarettes, to the detriment of global public health. It is essential that the United States contribute its expertise to international efforts to help the developing world avoid repeating the mistakes that have made tobacco our leading cause of preventable illness and premature death.

In the United States, we have learned from our mistakes. Tobacco consumption in the United States is on the decline overall, but this improvement has taken more than 4 decades. It need not be inevitable that the developing world repeat the US experience. Only through international collaboration can the projected epidemic of tobacco-related diseases that threatens lives—and economic expansion—in the developing world be avoided. Whether we, and the community of nations, have the will to adopt effective tobacco control strategies will determine our success in ending the tobacco pandemic.

Prevention Strategies Can Reduce Teen Smoking

by Paula M. Lantz, Peter D. Jacobson, and Kenneth E. Warner

About the authors: Paula M. Lantz, Peter D. Jacobson, and Kenneth E. Warner are with the Department of Health Management and Policy at the University of Michigan.

A large body of research shows that very few people in the United States initiate smoking or become habitual smokers after their teen years. At the present time, nearly 9 out of 10 current adult smokers (89%) started their habit before age 19. Although many tobacco prevention activities have focused on youth, smoking among U.S. adolescents actually rose throughout most of the 1990s, until declining somewhat in the past few years.

Given the epidemiology of smoking initiation, a great deal of policy and programmatic attention has been directed at youth smoking in the United States. In this article, we synthesize the burgeoning literature regarding efforts to discourage youth from smoking. For those areas in which there is empirical evidence from evaluations and other research studies, we summarize the state of the science regarding the impact or effectiveness of these general strategies. In addition, we also comment on emerging initiatives and interventions that have not yet been evaluated or have not received much attention in the peer-reviewed literature in an attempt to identify emerging trends and promising innovations.

School-Based Educational Interventions

A large number of school-based programs have been implemented during the past three decades. Most of these efforts target elementary school and/or middle school students. As described in a 1994 Institute of Medicine report, the majority of these programs have tended to be based on one of three main approaches. The first approach is an *information deficit* or *rational model* in which the program provides information about the health risks and negative consequences of tobacco, most often in a manner intended to arouse concern or fear. The primary premise of this approach is that youth are generally misinformed about the risks of smoking and that educating them about the health and social detriments of smoking will provide a deterrent.

The second major educational approach to youth tobacco prevention is an *affective education model* in which the program attempts to influence beliefs, attitudes, intentions, and norms related to tobacco use with a focus on enhancing self-esteem and values clarification. This type of program emphasizes initiation influences within an individual, recognizing that knowledge deficits are not the only factors associated with smoking initiation.

The third approach to tobacco prevention is based on a *social influence resistance model*, which emphasizes

> *"A state's commitment to the [tobacco control] program's intensity and comprehensiveness matters."*

the social environment as a critical factor in tobacco use. In addition to individual factors, influences outside of an individual, such as peer behavior or attitudes, and certain aspects of the environmental, familial, and cultural contexts, are considered to be of great importance. As such, this type of intervention focuses on building skills needed to recognize and resist negative influences, including recognition of advertising tactics and peer influences, communication and decision-making skills, and assertiveness.

The results of several individual evaluations and meta-analyses strongly suggest that educational programs based on the social influence resistance model are the most effective of the three approaches. Several individual studies and meta-analyses suggest that programs that incorporate a social influences model and focus on skills in recognizing and resisting social pressures have a modest but significant impact on both smoking initiation and level of use. Even so, the long-term impact of school-based educational interventions is of concern. It appears that the effects tend to dissipate with time, with effects generally persisting in the range of one to four years. Program "boosters" or subsequent interventions appear to enhance the staying power of the intervention effects, although the most appropriate content of and timing for these booster sessions is not known.

Community Interventions

The increased understanding of the combined effects of environmental, social, and cultural conditions on tobacco use has resulted in an emphasis on interventions that include comprehensive, community-based approaches. Such an approach targets multiple systems, institutions, or channels simultaneously, and employs multiple strategies. In general, community interventions have multiple components, and involve the use of community resources to influence both individual behavior and community norms or practices related to adolescent tobacco use. This includes the involvement of families, schools, community organizations, churches, businesses, the media, social service and health agencies, government, and law enforcement, with intervention strategies generally focused on making changes in both the environment and individual behavior.

Although community interventions take a variety of shapes, common elements among them include a shared emphasis on altering the social environment or social context in which tobacco products are obtained and used, and a shared goal of creating a social environment that is supportive of non-smoking and cessation. Some of the components of community interventions, such as mass media campaigns and youth access restrictions, are also implemented as stand-alone interventions, as described below.

While an increasing number of communities are attempting to influence youth tobacco use with multiple-component interventions, there are few published reports of evaluations with rigorous designs. The available research results, however, are encouraging in many cases. For example, a community intervention involving mass media, school-based education, parent education, community organizing, and policy advocacy in 15 communities in the Kansas City area was found to be effective in reducing tobacco, alcohol, and illicit drug use. Regarding tobacco use two years past the start of the intervention, the rate of smoking in the last month among youth was reported to be 19% in the intervention communities versus 29% in the control communities.

Working Together

School-based programs and community interventions involving parents, mass media, and community organizations appear to have a stronger impact over time when they work in tandem rather than as separate, stand-alone interventions. Mobilizing parents and community elements outside of the school (including the media) is seen as enhancing school-based interventions and increasing the potential for a lasting behavioral impact.

Although the results of a small number of controlled trials of community interventions attest to their ability to have an effect on youth smoking behavior, it is likely that broad-based community interventions alone are not sufficient to bring about a substantial and sustained decline in youth smoking. Community efforts, as symbolized by COMMIT (Community Intervention Trial for Smoking Cessation), ASSIST (American Stop Smoking Intervention Study), and other community interventions, likely need to be combined with stronger advocacy, taxation, media interventions, and policy formation and implementation, as discussed below.

Several state health departments (including those in California, Massachusetts, and Florida) have implemented comprehensive tobacco prevention and control programs that attempt to tackle youth tobacco using multiple interventions aimed at a number of different levels. Each of these programs targets several populations concurrently, and uses multiple channels to disseminate the message. These programs are comprehensive both in using a variety of strategies to reach their audiences, in incorporating multiple types of intervention (i.e., education, incentives, and regulation) at the state, regional and local levels, and attempting to have a strong policy component.

"Best practices" for this type of comprehensive tobacco control program were summarized in 2001 by the Centers for Disease Control and Prevention. While these programs are in the early stages of development and implementation in many states, early results suggest that these comprehensive models have significant potential for youth tobacco control. Early lessons drawn from state experiences are that more comprehensive, aggressive, and better funded state programs will lead to greater reductions in tobacco use than less intense efforts. In short, a state's commitment to the program's intensity and comprehensiveness matters.

Mass Media/Public Education

Mass media strategies have been used for broad-based public education regarding a variety of public health issues, including tobacco use prevention and control. Mass media efforts are viewed as particularly appropriate for reaching youth, who are often heavily exposed to and greatly interested in media messages. Youth have been the primary target of some hard-hitting and sophisticated anti-tobacco media campaigns in several communities and states, including California, Florida, and Massachusetts as a major part of their comprehensive tobacco control programs. In addition, the American Legacy Foundation (the independent foundation established as part of the 1998 multi-state settlement with the tobacco industry) has launched a large and aggressive anti-tobacco media campaign aimed at youth. Despite some encouraging information from Florida regarding a sharp decline in youth smoking, the impact of anti-tobacco media campaigns on smoking behavior among youth in general or specific subgroups is unknown. The few existing studies of the impact of mass media campaigns on youth smoking have shown varying results. Media campaigns that involve essential elements of social marketing and are theoretically driven may well have an effect on the attitudes and behaviors of youth regarding tobacco use, although the impact of such campaigns is challenging to evaluate and has not yet been demonstrated. The literature suggests that mass media interventions increase their chance of having an impact if the following conditions are met:

"The general consensus is that higher prices are an effective deterrent to youth smoking."

1) the campaign strategies are based on sound social marketing principles;
2) the effort is large and intense enough;
3) target groups are carefully differentiated;
4) messages for specific target groups resonate with "core values" of the group (rather than simply preach about the health risks of tobacco use), and

are based on empirical findings regarding the needs and interests of the group; and

5) the campaign is of sufficient duration.

Tobacco Advertising Restrictions

Cigarettes are a heavily advertised and marketed consumer product. There is great concern that tobacco advertising and marketing—including the distribution of promotional products such as clothing, sporting equipment, and gear for outdoor activities—are positively associated with youth smoking. A growing amount of research evidence suggests that youth awareness of tobacco marketing campaigns, receipt of free tobacco samples, and receipt of direct mail promotional paraphernalia are associated with smoking susceptibility and initiation.

The technical limitations of econometric approaches to estimating the effects of advertising on cigarette consumption, combined with a lack of studies on adolescent smoking make this literature of little use in trying to assess whether advertising affects smoking by adolescents.

Similarly, the potential effect of cigarette advertising restrictions or bans on adolescent smoking behavior also is unclear. Some states and municipalities have implemented restrictions regarding tobacco advertising. These types of bans are too new to have been evaluated yet, and the implementation of similar bans nationwide has been delayed because of legal challenges. Researchers, however, have concluded that total bans on tobacco advertising would likely have a greater impact than partial bans, because partial bans afford tobacco companies the opportunity to switch advertising expenditures to other promotional media and methods.

Youth Access Restrictions

In the past decade, the issue of youth access to tobacco products has received an explosion of attention. Policy action has been seen in a number of areas, including regulation of sellers, regulation of buyers, restrictions on the distribution of free products or samples (including coupons), and regulation of the means of tobacco sale (where and how it can be sold). The latter includes state and local efforts to restrict or totally ban tobacco sales via vending machines.

Federal Public Law 102-321, commonly referred to as the Synar amendment and enacted in 1991, stipulates that states must enforce laws restricting the sale and distribution of tobacco products to minors and must demonstrate success in reducing youth tobacco access or risk not receiving the full complement of block grant funding for the treatment and prevention of substance abuse. Although the Synar amendment has led to a number of developments in youth tobacco control, it is believed that few jurisdictions seriously enforce laws regarding the sale of tobacco to minors. This is important, because while laws regarding sales to minors appear to be rather benign in and of themselves, what seems to make a difference regarding illegal tobacco sales to minors is whether or not the laws are enforced.

Several controlled community intervention studies have demonstrated that increased enforcement of tobacco-sales laws can reduce illegal sales to minors. Unfortunately, however, the evidence that a reduction in sales actually translates into a reduction in tobacco consumption is limited. Several studies failed to look at the impact of enforcement interventions on smoking behavior. In studies that looked at both sales and behavior, the two did not always go hand in hand.

If the only or primary way in which youth gain access to cigarettes is through illegal sales, then we might expect the enforcement of youth access laws to have a powerful effect on smoking behavior. However, youth cite a number of "social sources" (such as family, friends, or even strangers) for their cigarettes as well as illegal purchase. Thus, what can be said with the evidence at hand is that youth access interventions can lead to a general reduction in illegal sales of cigarettes to minors. Whether this will translate into reduced and sustained reductions in youth tobacco use remains to be seen.

Tobacco Excise Taxes

Tobacco products are taxed by the federal government, states, and a few local governments. While generating revenue, tobacco taxation is also a policy that creates an economic disincentive to use tobacco. Theoretically, increasing the price of cigarettes through taxation could reduce adolescent cigarette consumption through three mechanisms:

1) some adolescents would quit smoking;
2) some would reduce the amount that they smoke; and
3) some would not start smoking in the first place.

The extent to which higher cigarette taxes will achieve these objectives depends upon how responsive smokers, and prospective smokers, are to price increases.

Studies of the elasticity of demand for cigarettes have followed a long tradition, dating back more than half a century. Most of these studies have focused on the adult or overall demand for cigarettes, with comparatively few focused on teenage cigarette demand. In regard to youth, the evidence on the degree to which teenagers are responsive to changes in cigarette prices is mixed, but the general consensus is that higher prices are an effective deterrent to youth smoking. That is, increasing the price of cigarettes leads to lower consumption by both adults and teenagers. Because cigarette price increases have been relatively small (i.e., under a dollar and, in many cases, just a few cents), it is difficult to predict with confidence the impact that a large price increase—such as a dollar or more per pack—would have on teenage cigarette consumption. The effects might be expected to be proportionately greater than those of a small tax increase.

Recent Innovations

The purpose of this section is to identify emerging trends and promising innovations in policy and programmatic responses to youth smoking. The majority of strategies described below have received no or only cursory evaluations. Thus, while some of these approaches may be compelling or appear to have promise, there is little to no empirical evidence to support claims about their worth or effectiveness at this time.

Smoking Cessation Interventions. The results of a number of descriptive studies and focus group studies suggest that many teen smokers are motivated to quit smoking. The impact of smoking cessation interventions among adolescents, however, is not well understood. None of the nicotine replacement therapies currently on the market have been approved for subjects under the age of 18. In addition, until very recently, formal smoking cessation programs were aimed exclusively at adults. An important recent trend, however, is an increase in the number of such smoking cessation programs now available for youth. Given the cost-effectiveness of smoking cessation interventions for adults, and the large number of addicted teenagers, research on cessation programs tailored to youth is an important area and should be a high priority.

> *"Research on cessation programs tailored to youth is an important area."*

Computer-Based Systems. An important emerging trend is the use of computer-based systems to communicate messages about tobacco to teens. Some of these innovations have been evaluated, but because most are in various stages of development and implementation we consider them under the category of new innovations. The advantages of these efforts, if successful, are their low cost and adolescent receptivity to computer-based information.

Peer-Based Interventions. A major trend in school-based interventions is the use of peer-education programs, such as Teens Against Tobacco Use. These programs train older students to become positive role models for middle and elementary school students. Many of these programs include a media literacy component through which teens learn how the tobacco industry's advertising savvy has manipulated and distorted information about tobacco.

Penalties for Possession and Use. A controversial response to youth tobacco use that has emerged is the increasing willingness of state and municipal policymakers to fine underage youth for using tobacco products. Tobacco control advocates have vociferously protested this approach as an attempt to shift attention away from vendors who sell tobacco products to minors. Regardless, this shift appears to be gaining momentum. Minors caught smoking or in possession of cigarettes can face a variety of penalties, ranging from a ticket or fine to suspension from school, denial of a driver's license; or any combination of these responses. Fines can also be combined with tobacco education or cessation classes. An additional important innovation to watch for in this area is the use of teen smoking courts.

School Policies. Schools may have their own smoking policies, which can apply even to those students over 18 years old. Penalties for violations include fines, smoking education and cessation classes, informing the student's parents, and suspension and/or expulsion. It appears that schools are increasingly willing to develop, implement, and enforce no-smoking policies. Recent school smoking policies seem to use a combination of punishments, rather than just fining or suspending students.

Restrictions on the Sale and Marketing of Tobacco Products. One way to restrict youth access to tobacco products is to physically remove the products from areas where youth can go. For example, recent restrictions on vending machines have been effective in removing them as a source of cigarettes for minors. In addition, the issue of billboard tobacco advertising was addressed in the 46-state settlement with the tobacco industry, which stipulated the removal of billboard advertisements by April 23, 1999. An emerging trend is to restrict self-service displays of cigarettes.

Direct Restrictions on Smoking. Policy efforts to restrict public smoking have proliferated since the 1980s. Such efforts include state and local restrictions on smoking in public facilities, outdoor spaces, worksites, hospitals, restaurants, bars, hotels,

> *"Youth smoking arises from some of the same family, peer, and community influences that are also important to [other forms of] risk-taking."*

and on airline flights. Some econometric studies of teenage and young adult smoking behavior have found evidence that clean indoor air laws reduce teenage cigarette consumption. Although the reasons why such laws may be effective in reducing youth smoking are unknown, one could speculate that they simply reduce the opportunities available for smoking. Alternatively, or perhaps in conjunction with these reduced opportunities, clean indoor air laws may be a useful vehicle for creating a cultural norm that suggests smoking is socially unacceptable.

Adolescent Risk Taking

Youth smoking occurs in a web of social relations that fosters many types of adolescent experimentation and that also may foster problem behaviors. Because of this social context, youth smoking arises from some of the same family, peer, and community influences that are also important to sexual risk-taking, crime and violence, and the initiation of harmful alcohol and illicit substance use. Existing prevention research regarding other adolescent problem behaviors therefore has potentially important implications for the design and evaluation of programs to curb youth smoking. Such interventions for older adolescents are often focused on improving academic skills. Many are also aimed at creating a sustained relationship with adult advisors or mentors who can provide social and emotional support while reinforcing appropriate social norms regarding substance abuse and other behaviors. An additional approach involves "family-focused" interventions.

No Magic Bullet

The most obvious conclusion from this review is that adolescent smoking prevention efforts have had mixed results, and that there is no "magic bullet" in terms of youth tobacco control on the horizon. As a result, advocating for a focus on youth smoking prevention and control is somewhat controversial. Some policy analysts have suggested that the focus of public policy should be to reduce teenage smoking initiation rates. Others have suggested that the focus on children will undermine the broader and likely more fruitful initiatives and programs needed to attack smoking and to promote cessation among adult habitual smokers.

From a practical perspective, these different policy views are not mutually exclusive. Both can be implemented simultaneously, and should be considered as complementary rather than competing strategies. From a public health perspective, we are appropriately concerned that the prevalence of youth smoking remains high despite the amount of resources already devoted to this problem and the wide array of interventions that have been tried. Yet, it is possible that without these interventions, rates of both experimental and habitual smoking among youth would be even higher.

Our review suggests a number of prevention strategies that are promising, especially if conducted in a coordinated way to take advantage of potential synergies across interventions. This includes such intervention strategies as media campaigns, teen cessation programs, community interventions that change the social context of smoking, and tobacco excise tax increases. Equally as important, there is great potential for these interventions to be cost-effective. Even modest gains from prevention and cessation efforts could lead to substantial reductions in the morbidity and mortality costs of smoking. We believe that previous calls for tobacco control efforts that are "youth centered" remain relevant and critically important as we move into the 21st century.

This review suggests that there are a number of interventions and strategies that deserve further consideration, dissemination, and evaluation. The resources available through the settlement with the tobacco industry provide an unprecedented opportunity to invest in youth tobacco control. Thus, we strongly advocate that this opportunity be seized and that significant state resources—along with other resources—be devoted to expanding, improving and evaluating tobacco prevention and control activities among youth.

Nicotine Replacement Therapy Can Reduce Smoking

by Jonathan Foulds

About the author: *Jonathan Foulds is a senior lecturer of psychology at the University of Surrey in England.*

About two thirds of smokers in the UK say that they would like to quit and, at any one time, around a quarter are actively planning to give up.

Among adult smokers, 80 per cent have already made an unsuccessful attempt to stop smoking and, with an almost complete lack of dedicated smoking cessation services in the NHS [National Health Service], many smokers perceive the pharmacist as the most accessible source of advice and help for stopping smoking.

Aids to Giving Up

Pharmacy shelves contain a wide array of products intended to help smokers reduce their health risks.

These include dummy cigarettes, 'aromatherapy' products, herbal cigarettes, cigarette filters, licensed medications (e.g. Nicobrevin and nicotine gum, patch, nasal spray and inhalator) and unlicensed nicotine-containing preparations, e.g. Stoppers.

Of all these methods, only the licensed nicotine replacement therapies (NRTs) are backed up by solid evidence from controlled trials which demonstrate their safety and efficacy.

These studies suggest that smokers are approximately twice as likely to succeed in stopping smoking if they use NRT, compared with placebo.

NRT helps smokers to quit by reducing the severity of nicotine withdrawal symptoms (bad mood, poor concentration, hunger) during the first few weeks, and also by reducing the severity of craving for a cigarette.

Excerpted from "Stubbing It Out," by Jonathan Foulds, *Chemist & Druggist*, February 18, 1998. Copyright © 1998 Miller Freeman PLC Chemist & Druggist. Reprinted with permission of *Chemist & Druggist*.

Assessment

In order to judge the appropriate intervention for each client, the pharmacist should carry out a basic assessment of the smoker's motivation and dependence.

Motivation can be assessed by asking two simple questions:

a) Would you give up smoking altogether, if you could do so easily?

b) How much do you want to stop smoking altogether?

Answers to these questions can help classify patients according to their 'stage of change' as follows:

• precontemplation: not seriously thinking about stopping
• contemplation: seriously thinking about quitting in the next six months
• preparation: planning to quit in the next month
• action: not currently smoking, having quit in the last six months
• maintenance: quit smoking over six months ago.

Smokers who are clear that they very much want to stop smoking (those in the 'preparation' stage) should be encouraged to arrange a quit date (i.e. the day when they will stop smoking completely).

Those who are a bit more hesitant may require their motivation to be boosted. This can be achieved by (a) providing them with information which emphasises that they can succeed and that help is available, and (b) providing accurate information about their own personal health benefits from stopping smoking. . . .

Dependence

Nicotine dependence can similarly be assessed by two simple questions:

a) How many cigarettes do you typically smoke each day?

b) How soon after waking up do you smoke your first cigarette of the day?

Those smoking less than ten cigarettes per day and who wait over an hour before their first cigarette of the day are only mildly nicotine dependent and are unlikely to benefit from NRT.

They should be advised that their chances of success are good if they choose a quit date, get rid of all their tobacco the evening before, and try to quit completely from that day.

"Only the licensed nicotine replacement therapies are backed up by solid evidence . . . [that] demonstrate[s] their safety and efficacy."

Those who smoke 20 or more cigarettes each day and who smoke their first cigarette within 30 minutes of waking are highly addicted to nicotine and should strongly be advised to use a high dose of NRT (4mg nicotine gum or nicotine nasal spray probably being most appropriate).

Those who smoke between ten and 19 cigarettes per day could choose from 2mg nicotine gum, full strength nicotine patches or the nicotine inhalator according to their own preferences and requirements.

Each NRT product has its own advantages and disadvantages. For example, the patch has the important advantage of being easy to use (simply apply to the skin once per day) and so guarantees that the smoker will receive a therapeutic dose of nicotine.

However, because of its easy 'once a day' application, there is nothing for the smoker to do with their hands or when they feel a craving for a cigarette.

Other important advantages of the patch are its relatively good side effect profile (mild skin reddening and itching being the most common symptoms) and the fact that it is almost completely non-addictive.

The nasal spray (which is only available on prescription) is at the opposite end of the spectrum. It has to be used regularly throughout the day and has the advantage of providing fast delivery of nicotine when the smoker needs it.

However, it is typically perceived as having a rather harsh irritant effect on the nose during the first few days of use (producing effects not unlike those resulting from sniffing pepper) and so compliance may be a problem, particularly for those who are not highly motivated.

The most recent addition to the NRT portfolio is the Nicorette Inhalator, which was launched in the UK as an OTC [over-the-counter] product in December 1997. This device consists of a plastic mouthpiece shaped like a cigarette, and a number of nicotine-containing cartridges.

The smoker puffs on the mouthpiece, and the nicotine vapour is absorbed via the lining of the mouth and upper airways (similar absorption profile to nicotine gum).

> *"Smokers who are clear that they very much want to stop smoking . . . should be encouraged to arrange a quit date."*

The main perceived advantage of this product (other than its current novelty value) is that it more closely replaces the behavioural and sensory aspects of smoking.

The main problems with NRT in the over-the-counter arena are cost (usually slightly cheaper than the cost of cigarettes for a pack-a-day smoker), side effects (usually mild but irritating) and under-dosing.

In an attempt to reduce the cost and the side-effects, smokers frequently fail to take anything like the recommended dose of these products and consequently may not reap the benefits which have been demonstrated in clinical trials (reduced withdrawal symptoms and increased chances of achieving long term tobacco abstinence).

The Nicorette Inhalator

The new Nicorette Inhalator is a good case in point here. The starter pack costs around 5.95 pounds and contains the mouthpiece, holder and six cartridges. Six cartridges is the minimum recommended dose for one day, and ideally the smoker should use each one for one to three 20-minute sessions.

The first few puffs on the Inhalator typically produce mild coughing and throat irritation and so it is not surprising for clients to try to reduce both their costs and irritant effects by using less than the recommended dose, or even trying to quit using only the starter pack.

It is therefore crucial to explain to clients that the initial irritant effects will ease after a few days of use and that it will only reduce their craving if used regularly. It is also worth pointing out that the weekly pack (containing 42 cartridges) is proportionally cheaper (just under 20 pounds).

Compliance with NRT and the likelihood of successful abstinence are both improved by forming a collaborative and supportive relationship between the patient [and the pharmacist].

> *"The main perceived advantage of [the Nicorette Inhalator] . . . is that it more closely replaces the behavioural and sensory aspects of smoking."*

The process of assessing the client's dependence and motivation, advising on appropriate aids, and suggesting that they come back within a week in order to monitor progress, need not take much time but may make the difference between success and failure.

Although other forms of assistance such as information leaflets, 'Quitline' and 'No Smoking Day' are difficult to evaluate formally, they all provide additional advice and support which will improve the smoker's chances, and so are well worth incorporating into pharmacy-based smoking cessation interventions.

Finally, it is worth bearing in mind that smoking, like other addictive behaviours, is subject to high relapse rates in those trying to give up.

Thus, the pharmacist and pharmacy assistants will inevitably see more patients who fail than succeed on their first attempt.

This can sometimes be demoralising and lead to the feeling that nothing works. However, pharmacists are now the main providers of advice and medications that have proven efficacy, and if a little time is spent assessing and advising patients, then their chances of succeeding will roughly double.

Organizations to Contact

The editors have compiled the following list of organizations concerned with the issues debated in this book. The descriptions are derived from materials provided by the organizations. All have publications or information available for interested readers. The list was compiled on the date of publication of the present volume; the information provided here may change. Be aware that many organizations take several weeks or longer to respond to inquiries, so allow as much time as possible.

Action on Smoking and Health (ASH)
2013 H St. NW, Washington, DC 20006
(202) 659-4310
website: www.ash.org

Action on Smoking and Health promotes the rights of nonsmokers and works to protect them from the harms of smoking. ASH worked to eliminate tobacco ads from radio and television and to ban smoking in airplanes, buses, and many public places. The organization publishes the bimonthly newsletter *ASH Smoking and Health Review* and fact sheets on a variety of topics, including teen smoking, passive smoking, and nicotine addiction.

American Cancer Society
1599 Clifton Rd. NE, Atlanta, GA 30329
(800) ACS-2345 (227-2345)
website: www.cancer.org

The American Cancer Society is one of the primary organizations in the United States devoted to educating the public about cancer and to funding cancer research. The society spends a great deal of its resources on educating the public about the dangers of smoking and on lobbying for antismoking legislation. The American Cancer Society makes available hundreds of publications, ranging from reports and surveys to position papers.

American Council on Science and Health (ACSH)
1995 Broadway, 2nd Fl., New York, NY 10023-5860
(212) 362-7044 • fax: (212) 362-4919
e-mail: acsh@acsh.org • website: www.acsh.org

ACSH is a consumer education group concerned with issues related to food, nutrition, chemicals, pharmaceuticals, lifestyle, the environment, and health. It publishes the quarterly newsletter *Priorities* as well as the booklets *The Tobacco Industry's Use of Nicotine as a Drug* and *Marketing Cigarettes to Kids*.

American Lung Association (ALA)
1740 Broadway, New York, NY 10019-4374
(212) 315-8700 • fax: (212) 265-5642
e-mail: info@lungusa.org • website: www.lungusa.org

Founded in 1904, the American Lung Association is the oldest voluntary health agency in the United States. It is dedicated to the prevention, cure, and control of all types of lung disease, including asthma, emphysema, tuberculosis, and lung cancer. ALA's mission is to prevent lung disease and to promote lung health.

American Medical Association (AMA)
515 N. State St., Chicago, IL 60610
(312) 464-5000
website: www.ama-assn.org

The AMA is the largest professional association for medical doctors. It helps set standards for medical education and practices and is a powerful lobby in Washington for physicians' interests. It publishes the monthly *JAMA,* the *Journal of the American Medical Association.*

Americans for Nonsmokers' Rights
2530 San Pablo Ave., Suite J, Berkeley, CA 94702
(510) 841-3032 • fax: (510) 841-3071
e-mail: anr@no-smoke.org • website: www.no-smoke.org

Americans for Nonsmokers' Rights seeks to protect the rights of nonsmokers in the workplace and other public settings. It works with the American Nonsmokers' Rights Foundation, which promotes smoking prevention, nonsmokers' rights, and public education about involuntary smoking. The organization publishes the quarterly newsletter *ANR Update*, the book *Clearing the Air*, and the guidebook *How to Butt In: Teens Take Action.*

Canadian Council for Tobacco Control (CCTC)
75 Albert St., Suite 508, Ottawa, ON K1P 5E7 Canada
(800) 267-5234 • (613) 567-3050 • fax: (613) 567-5695
e-mail: info-services@cctc.ca • website: www.cctc.ca

The CCTC works to ensure a healthier society, free from addiction and involuntary exposure to tobacco products. It promotes a comprehensive tobacco control program involving educational, social, fiscal, and legislative interventions. It publishes several fact sheets, including *Promoting a Lethal Product* and *The Ban on Smoking on School Property: Successes and Challenges.*

Cato Institute
1000 Massachusetts Ave. NW, Washington, DC 20001
(202) 842-0200
website: www.cato.org

The institute is a libertarian public policy research foundation dedicated to limiting the control of government and protecting individual liberty. Its quarterly magazine *Regulation* has published articles and letters questioning the accuracy of EPA studies on the dangers of secondhand smoke. The Cato Journal is published by the institute three times a year and the Cato Policy Analysis occasional papers are published periodically.

Children Opposed to Smoking Tobacco (COST)
Mary Volz School, 509 W. 3rd Ave., Runnemede, NJ 08078
e-mail: costkids@costkids.org • website: www.costkids.org

COST was founded in1996 by a group of middle school students committed to keeping tobacco products out of the hands of children. Much of the organization's efforts are spent fighting the tobacco industry's advertising campaigns directed at children and teenagers. Articles, such as *Environmental Tobacco Smoke, What Is a Parent to Do?*, and *What You Can Do*, are available on its website.

Coalition on Smoking OR Health
1150 Connecticut Ave. NW, Suite 820, Washington, DC 20036
(202) 452-1184

Formed by the American Lung Association, the American Heart Association, and the American Cancer Society, the coalition has worked to revise warning labels on tobacco products and to ban smoking in public places. It seeks to restrict advertising of tobacco products, to increase tobacco taxes, to regulate tobacco products, and to prohibit youths' access to tobacco products. It publishes the report *Tobacco Use: An American Crisis,* the briefing kits *Leveling the Playing Field* and *Saving Lives and Raising Revenue,* as well as fact sheets and several annual publications.

Competitive Enterprise Institute (CEI)
1001 Connecticut Ave. NW, Suite 1250, Washington, DC 20036
(202) 331-1010 • fax: (202) 331-0640
e-mail: info@cei.org • website: www.cei.org

The institute is a pro–free market public interest group involved in a wide range of issues, including tobacco. CEI questions the validity and accuracy of Environmental Protection Agency studies that report the dangers of secondhand smoke. Its publications include books, monographs, and policy studies, and the monthly newsletter *CEI Update.*

drkoop.com
225 Arizona Ave., Suite 250, Santa Monica, CA 90401
(310) 395-5700 • fax: (310) 395-3800
e-mail: feedback@drkoop.com • website: www.drkoop.com/tobacco

Based on the vision of former U.S. surgeon general C. Everett Koop, drkoop.com is a consumer-focused interactive website that provides users with comprehensive health-care information on a wide variety of subjects, including tobacco. The organization publishes reports, fact sheets, press releases, and books, including *The No-Nag, No-Guilt, Do-It-Your-Own Way Guide to Quitting Smoking.*

Environmental Protection Agency (EPA)
Indoor Air Quality Information Clearinghouse
PO Box 37133, Washington, DC 20013-7133
(800) 438-4318 • (703) 356-4020 • fax: (703) 356-5386
e-mail: iaqinfo@aol.com • website: www.epa.gov/iaq

The EPA is the agency of the U.S. government that coordinates actions designed to protect the environment. It promotes indoor air quality standards that reduce the dangers of secondhand smoke. The EPA publishes and distributes reports such as *Respiratory Health Effects of Passive Smoking: Lung Cancer and Other Disorders* and *What You Can Do About Secondhand Smoke as Parents, Decisionmakers, and Building Occupants.*

Fight Ordinances & Restrictions to Control & Eliminate Smoking (FORCES)
PO Box 14347, San Francisco, CA 94114-0347
(415) 675-0157
e-mail: info@forces.org • website: www.forces.org

FORCES fights against smoking ordinances and restrictions designed to eventually eliminate smoking, and it works to increase public awareness of smoking-related legislation. It opposes any state or local ordinance it feels is not fair to those who choose to smoke. Although FORCES does not advocate smoking, it asserts that an individual has the right to choose to smoke and that smokers should be accommodated where and when possible. FORCES publishes *Tobacco Weekly* as well as many articles.

Food and Drug Administration (FDA)
5600 Fishers Ln., Rockville, MD 20857
(888) INFO-FDA (463-6332)
website: www.fda.gov

An agency of the U.S. government charged with protecting the health of the public against impure and unsafe foods, drugs, cosmetics, and other potential hazards, the FDA has sought the regulation of nicotine as a drug and has investigated manipulation of nicotine levels in cigarettes by the tobacco industry. It provides copies of congressional testimony given in the debate over regulation of nicotine.

Foundation for Economic Education
30 S. Broadway, Irvington-on-Hudson, NY 10533
(914) 591-7230 • fax: (914) 591-8910
e-mail: fee@fee.org • web address: www.fee.org

The foundation promotes private property rights, the free market economic system, and limited government. Its monthly journal, the *Freeman,* has published articles opposing regulation of the tobacco industry.

Group Against Smoking Pollution (GASP)
PO Box 632, College Park, MD 20741-0632
(301) 459-4791
e-mail: gasp@gasp-pgh.org • website: www.gasp-pgh.org

Consisting of nonsmokers adversely affected by tobacco smoke, GASP works to promote the rights of nonsmokers, to educate the public about the problems of secondhand smoke, and to encourage the regulation of smoking in public places. The organization provides information and referral services and distributes educational materials, buttons, posters, and bumper stickers. GASP publishes booklets and pamphlets such as *The Nonsmokers' Bill of Rights* and *The Nonsmokers' Liberation Guide.*

KidsHealth.org
The Nemours Foundation Center for Children's Health Media
1600 Rockland Rd., Wilmington, DE 19803
(302) 651-4000 • fax: (302) 651-4077
e-mail: info@KidsHealth.org • website: www.KidsHealth.org

The mission of KidsHealth.org is to help families make informed decisions about children's health by creating the highest quality health media. It utilizes cutting-edge technology and a wealth of trusted medical resources to provide the best in pediatric health information. Its teen section covers a wide variety of issues, including teen smoking. *How to Raise Non-Smoking Kids* and *Smoking: Cutting Through the Hype* are two of its numerous publications.

Libertarian Party
1528 Pennsylvania Ave. SE, Washington, DC 20003
website: www.lp.org

The goal of this political party is to ensure respect for individual rights. It opposes regulation of smoking. The party publishes the bimonthly *Libertarian Party News* and periodic *Issue Papers.*

National Center for Tobacco-Free Kids/Campaign for Tobacco-Free Kids
1707 L St. NW, Suite 800, Washington, DC 20036
(800) 284-KIDS (284-5437)
e-mail: info@tobaccofreekids.org • website: www.tobaccofreekids.org

The National Center for Tobacco-Free Kids/Campaign for Tobacco-Free Kids is the largest private initiative ever launched to protect children from tobacco addiction. The center works in partnership with the American Cancer Society, American Heart Association, American Medical Association, the National PTA, and over one hundred other health, civic, corporate, youth, and religious organizations. Among the center's publications are press releases, reports, and fact sheets, including *Tobacco Use Among Youth, Tobacco Marketing to Kids,* and *Smokeless (Spit) Tobacco and Kids.*

Reason Foundation
3415 S. Sepulveda Blvd., Suite 400, Los Angeles, CA 90034
(310) 391-2245
website: www.reason.org

The Reason Foundation is a libertarian research and education foundation that works to promote free markets and limited government. It publishes the monthly *Reason* magazine, which occasionally contains articles opposing the regulation of smoking.

SmokeFree Educational Services, Inc.
375 South End Ave., Suite 32F, New York, NY 10280
(212) 912-0960
website: www.smokefreeair.org

This organization works to educate youth on the relationship between smoking and health. It publishes the quarterly newsletter *SmokeFree Air* and the book *Kids Say Don't Smoke* and distributes posters, stickers, and videotapes.

The Tobacco Institute
1875 I St. NW, Washington, DC 20006
website: www.tobaccoinstitute.com

The institute is the primary national lobbying organization for the tobacco industry. The institute argues that the dangers of smoking have not been proven and opposes regulation of tobacco. It provides the public with general information on smoking issues.

Tobacco Merchants Association of the United States
PO Box 8019, Princeton, NJ 08543-8019
(609) 275-4900 • fax: (609) 275-8379
e-mail: tma@tma.org • website: www.tma.org

The association represents manufacturers of tobacco products; tobacco leaf dealers, suppliers, and distributors; and others related to the tobacco industry. It tracks statistics on the sale and distribution of tobacco and informs its members of this information through the following periodicals: the weekly newsletters *Executive Summary, World Alert,* and *Tobacco Weekly;* the biweekly *Leaf Bulletin* and *Legislative Bulletin;* the monthly *Trademark Report* and *Tobacco Barometer: Smoking, Chewing & Snuff;* and the quarterly newsletter *Issues Monitor.* The association has a reference library, offers on-line services, and provides economic, statistical, media-tracking, legislative, and regulatory information.

Tobacco Products Liability Project (TPLP)
Tobacco Control Resource Center
Northeastern University School of Law
400 Huntington Ave., Boston, MA 02115-5098
(617) 373-2026 • fax: (617) 373-3672
e-mail: tobacco@bigfoot.com

Founded in 1984 by doctors, academics, and attorneys, TPLP studies, encourages, and coordinates product liability suits in order to publicize the effects of smoking on health. It publishes the monthly newsletter *Tobacco on Trial.*

Bibliography

Books

Muhammed Al-Jibaly — *Smoking—A Social Poison*. Anchorage, AK: Al-Kitaab & As-Sunnah, 1999.

C.T. Bollinger and Karl-Olov Fagerstrom — *The Tobacco Epidemic*. Basel, Switzerland: S. Karger AG, 1997.

Allan Brandt — *Rise and Fall of the Cigarette: A Cultural History of Smoking in the U.S.* New York: Basic Books, 1999.

Sean Connolly — *Tobacco*. Katy, TX: Heinemann Library, 2000.

Gina DeAngelis, Stephen L. Jaffe, and Barry R. McCaffrey — *Nicotine and Cigarettes*. Broomall, PA: Chelsea House, 1999.

Bill Dodds — *1,440 Reasons to Quit Smoking: (One for Every Minute of the Day)*. Minnetonka, MN: Meadowbrook, 2000.

William L. Fibkins — *What Schools Should Do to Help Kids Stop Smoking*. Larchmont, NY: Eye on Education, 2000.

Bonnie B. Graves — *Tobacco Use*. Mankato, MN: Capstone, 2000.

Emma Haughton — *A Right to Smoke?* New York: Watts, 1997.

Hugh High — *Does Advertising Increase Smoking? Economic, Free Speech, and Advertising Bans*. London: Institute of Economic Affairs, 1999.

Arlene B. Hirschfelder — *Kick Butts*. Lanham, MD: Scarecrow, 2001.

Peter D. Jacobson — *Tobacco Control Laws: Implementation and Enforcement*. Santa Monica, CA: RAND, 1997.

Elizabeth Keyishan — *Everything You Need to Know About Smoking*. Brookshire, TX: Rosen, 1999.

Barbara B. Lloyd, Sheena McGrellis, Sean Arnold, Kevin Lucas, and Janet Holland — *Smoking in Adolescence: Images and Identities*. New York: Routledge, 1998.

Bibliography

Joan Vos V. MacDonald   *Tobacco and Nicotine Drug Dangers.* Springfield, NJ: Enslow, 2000.

Mike A. Males   *Smoked: Why Joe Camel Is Still Smiling.* Monroe, ME: Common Courage, 1999.

Daniel McMillan   *Teen Smoking: Understanding the Risks.* Springfield, NJ: Enslow, 1997.

Lynn Michell   *Growing Up in Smoke.* London: Pluto, 1999.

Barbara Miller   *How to Quit Smoking Even If You Don't Want To.* Victoria, British Columbia: Trafford, 2000.

Barbara A. Moe   *Teen Smoking and Tobacco Use.* Springfield, NJ: Enslow, 2000.

Corky Newton   *Generation Risk: How to Protect Your Teenager from Smoking and Other Dangerous Behavior.* New York: M. Evans, 2001.

Don Oakley   *Slow Burn: The Great American Anti-Smoking Scam (and Why It Will Fail).* New York: Eyrie, 1999.

Jeffrey A. Schaler and Magda E. Schaler   *Smoking: Who Has the Right?* Amherst, NY: Prometheus, 1998.

Paul Slovic   *Smoking: Risk, Perception, and Policy.* London: Sage, 2001.

Jacob Sullum   *For Your Own Good: The Anti-Smoking Crusade and the Tyranny of Public Health.* New York: Free Press, 1998.

Elizabeth M. Whelan   *Cigarettes: What the Warning Label Doesn't Tell You: The First Comprehensive Guide to the Health Consequences of Smoking.* Amherst, NY: Prometheus, 1997.

Adam Winters and Michael A. Sommers   *Tobacco and Your Mouth: The Incredibly Disgusting Story.* Brookshire, TX: Rosen, 2000.

Mark L. Witten and Ronald R. Watson   *Environmental Tobacco Smoke.* Boca Raton, FL: CRC, 2000.

World Health Organization   *Tobacco or Health: A Global Status Report.* Geneva: World Health Organization, 1997.

Periodicals

Community Pharmacy   "Killers in the Mist," February 1998.

David W. Cowles   "The Price of Smoking," *Newsweek*, February 1, 1999.

Barbara Dority   "The Rights of Joe Camel and the Marlboro Man," *Humanist*, January/February 1997.

John Elvin   "Individual Rights Going Up in Smoke," *Insight on the News*, March 5, 2001.

Greg Gutfield   "I Smoke," *Men's Health*, June 1, 1999.

Gayle M.B. Hanson   "Tobacco and Liberty," *Insight on the News*, March 16, 1998.

| Marianne Lavelle | "Teen Tobacco Wars," *U.S. News & World Report*, February 7, 2000. |

Robert A. Levy and Rosalind B. Marimont — "Lies, Damned Lies, & 400,000 Smoking-Related Deaths," *Regulation*, 1998.

Kathryn Marsden — "K Is for Kick the Smoking Habit," *Beauty Counter*, March 1999.

Medical & Healthcare Marketplace Guide — "Addiction—Combating the Tobacco Epidemic," 1999.

William D. Novelli — "'Don't Smoke,' Buy Marlboro," *British Medical Journal*, May 8, 1999.

Laura A. Peracchio and David Luna — "The Development of an Advertising Campaign to Discourage Smoking Initiation Among Children and Youth," *Journal of Advertising*, Fall 1998.

Alberta Peugeot, Cathy Urquhart Anderson, and Sharon Fruh — "Teenage Tobacco Use," *Nurse Practitioner*, September 1999.

Michael Reznicek — "Smokers Aren't Victims," *Weekly Standard*, August 18, 1997.

Lydia Saad — "A Half-Century of Polling on Tobacco: Most Don't Like Smoking but Tolerate It," *Public Perspective*, August 1998.

Dick Teresi — "Second Chance Smoke (or, How I Longed to Light Up at 50)," *Forbes*, November 17, 1997.

W. Kip Viscusi — "Smoke and Mirrors: Understanding the New Scheme for Cigarette Regulation," *Brookings Review*, Winter 1998.

Caroline White — "Smoking in Public Should Be Restricted," *British Medical Journal*, March 21, 1998.

Index